End to End SaaS Serviceability, Metrics, Monitoring, and Alerting

Eamon Maguire

ISBN:
9781521854433

CONTENTS

About the Author

An older brother with a penchant for all things computer first introduced a middle school aged kid that would later to go on to write this book to the world of computing and programming. During the Stone Age, prior to the spread of what would later become the internet from CERN, a plethora of different operating systems and hardware configurations littered the nascent personal computing market. Our household had several different models in various stages of undress: a Tandy, RadioShack's entry into the market; an Apple IIe, the monochrome ASCII graphic equipped precursor to the Mac, complete with an integrated BASIC IDE; the ahead of its time Amiga 500, one of the few computers of the era to sport a full GUI based OS; and an early PC, the DOS equipped beast that would later become one of only two serious competitors left in the in personal computing market.

If one hoped to play any of the games on these computers, one necessarily had to learn the command line, and in several different flavors, as all of these computers had different operating systems, command line conventions, file naming conventions, different exception and error return codes, different manners in which to install upgrades to memory and hardware, different ways to boot to BIOS, and so on.

In the pre-internet days, we also had something known as a bulletin board system or "BBS" for short. These were remotely hosted text-based terminal programs that gave access to text based multi-user door games, message forums, and collections of home brewed and open source software. In order to access all this good stuff at a few kilo of baud width, one had to be familiar with the terminal commands, ATDT and the like. Without them, you couldn't get the modem to chirp, crackle, beep and eventually connect over the phone line to play your daily quota of turns in Legend of the Red Dragon or BRE (I slayed at that game).

After getting familiar with all of this for the sake of amusement, my older brother pointed out you could boot the Apple IIe into BASIC mode, and write and run your very own programs. I learned how to write some simple programs, and took this knowledge to the school's library that also used the ubiquitous Apple IIe. I would boot the computers into BASIC mode, and replace the card catalog's welcome prompt with a simple program that would prompt the user for their name. For most users there was a generic friendly response, but there was a small subset of users that received a custom insult message upon entering their name (trust me they were jerks). The librarians weren't as amused as I felt they should be, but hey, they should have locked down booting into BASIC; that is a security risk!

The internet rose rapidly, and I took my first formal web programming classes in the late 90s, learning HTML, CSS, and Visual Basic. Unfortunately, the dot-com crash leveled the software industry at that point; bad times. It would be a number of years till I returned to academia to pursue a computer science degree.

After obtaining a liberal arts junior college degree, I worked in various mundane jobs as I had virtually every day since I was old enough to legally do so. Retail, food service, and restaurant management. Later I obtained some medical certifications and worked as a lab technician, collecting blood samples and performing laboratory tests for patients suffering from varying degrees of sickness and injury at local hospitals, including our local VA hospital.

Finally, I returned to school by enrolling in the highly regarded University of Washington computer science program. I obtained a bachelors of science, a big data technologies certification, and also enrolled in graduate school, all through UW's computer science program.

During my junior year, I worked helping professors and graduate students with research into machine learning and data provenance. I also got my first paying gig as a firmware engineer at a local startup. It was an awesome opportunity to be engineer number one working directly with the two founding engineers - one of whom had a PHD in computer science - that collectively had nearly forty years of industry experience working for fortune 500 companies.

I also got the full-stack experience; I soldered Wi-Fi chips to embedded systems, used oscilloscopes to check pin signals, wrote efficient C++ programs that manipulated registers, opened sockets to web services, read in data byte by byte, and all with mere kilobytes of memory. We topped it all off with a suite of front-end services that queried SQL databases and generated views using C#.

Upon graduating, I worked at Amazon in the third party marketplace writing full-stack applications using Java Spring backend services, Dynamo DB and SQL, various front-end languages to generate views and interact with backend services, and a gaggle of monitoring, analytics, and troubleshooting tools. From there I went on to Cisco Systems where I worked on a variety of cloud applications relating to collaboration, IVR, VOIP, chat bots, and all the associated metrics, analytics, and troubleshooting tools.

Throughout the course of these various projects and on-call rotations, I've acquired a broad, diverse set of experiences with respect to distributed systems. I've experienced bugs and issues in a plethora of different scenarios, at a variety of scales, and have been on the hook for some potentially very serious outcomes if things were not restored to a functional state in short order. I've taken this experience, and done my best to help other engineers get out of the downtime/degraded service hot seat as quickly as possible, or better yet to avoid it all together.

About this Book

Consider that at the time this book was published Amazon Web Services had been in service only eleven years, Microsoft Azure had been in service only seven years, and Google Cloud Platform just five years. Prior to the advent of these solutions, distributed systems certainly existed, but we had just started the Smartphone revolution with the release of the first iPhone in 2007. Put simply, systems of the scale and scope we see now simply did not exist in any appreciably similar form prior to less than a decade ago.

While a decade is like a hundred years in tech-time, there are bound to be growing pains; we're immature when it comes to cloud computing at scale. No one programs in BASIC anymore, and you'd be hard pressed to find a job writing COBOL. That's not to say it was wrong or naive to have learned these languages, or to have had a genuine belief they would persist and be forever used like SQL; however, we need to eventually recognize that we're trying to fit a square peg in a round hole.

In my experience, there tend to be two approaches to applying Serviceability and monitoring at scale: best effort, and head in the sand. In the best effort case, smart, effective engineers come up with their best guess effort at what it takes to make an application bulletproof at scale, and they hit a few dingers, but they end up writing Ada or Fortran instead of SQL. The other approach is to buy one of those all-in-one solutions from the tech equivalent of the snake oil salesman. Your engineers learn how to game the threshold system, and stick their heads in the sand pretending there isn't a problem until you have so much tech debt, and your on-call shifts are so miserable, you start losing engineers to burnout and frustration.

Neither of these options is going to work. Very smart people have made best efforts, and their tools are relegated to the scrap heap of tech history. Serviceability, metrics, monitoring, and alerting at scale in a distributed system is insidiously complicated, and more often than not done very, very wrong.

Whether you're an experienced engineer that considers themselves a full-stack developer, a newbie, an engineering manager, or a shot caller in your business unit, you are unlikely to come up with the timeless, solid solution to your serviceability needs you want. It is also nearly as improbable that the snake oil salesman that offered to give you the revitalizing all-in-one oh-so-simple plug-in-and-go solution really has the goods.

While any serviceability solution is a living, breathing thing that must constantly be improved and reexamined, you don't have to fumble in the dark, and it is unlikely that in today's crowded SaaS marketplace you could survive for long if you did; your customer will find another solution if you can't get Serviceability right. I can give you the tools to allow you to design a framework that you can understand, justify, rationalize, expand, and own. A good Serviceability, metrics, monitoring, and alerting framework can help you make the lives of your on-call engineers less stressful, keep your project managers happy, and the customers coming back for more servings of SaaS.

General Serviceability Principles

Serviceability in the context of software systems, in a general sense, is a well-defined theoretical concept. In lofty, high-level detail, Serviceability represents the ability of an engineer or other related information technology worker to diagnose, triage, and ultimately repair unforeseen bad system states of varying severity.

Outside the academic, coarse-grained, theoretical conception of Serviceability, however, lies a great deal of variance; technologies are numerous and diverse, languages, architectures, and use cases vary dramatically as well. The Serviceability of software and hardware running a nuclear power plant has fundamentally different needs than the latest edition of solitaire on your mobile device.

From a technological point of view, due to limitations and restrictions with certain varieties of systems, the amount of time needed to solve, triage, and ultimately resolve bad system states can vary wildly. For example, a defect in an EEPROM device, where byte code is burned into the device's memory, would naturally have a much longer and more involved process to resolve emergent issues than an Apache Log server running on the latest and greatest cloud infrastructure.

I recall being engineer one at a local startup working with a Wi-Fi enabled embedded device. There were a number of issues we faced early on in the process. Some of these issues were inherent to embedded device development generally, others related to the fact that we were marrying cutting edge chips that had never been used together in a low cost consumer device before, and some issues were due to a lack of process as we were an immature company at this point.

We experienced vexing transient bugs. We'd have garbage control characters appearing on the OLED display, controllers attached to heating elements wouldn't shut down, and the elements would literally explode; we'd hear a loud pop, and go back to the lab and smell the acrid coolant vapor hanging in the air.

The memory and processing limitations of the embedded system severely limited our ability to add debug statements, and other test harnesses simply didn't exist for our particular hardware. We'd hack and cobble together various pieces of similar test frameworks to get something, anything, from the system. We'd set up the oscilloscope, and monitor the signals from the control pins, and everything, absolutely everything, checked out; it all looked fine.

We set up a mockup of the actual device, sans the exploding heating elements, and ran the embedded board in what was as close to the native conditions as we could; still nothing. Finally, someone had the idea to check the magnetic fields generated by the pumps, one of the elements not included in our mocked up test device.

We found that indeed, the electro-magnetic interference from the pumps was so strong that it had been affecting the embedded device's signals to the heat pumps. We added more shielding, and lo and behold, the issue vanished. This process took months of late nights.

The moral of the story is, not being able to tell what is happening in your system can lead to a lot of late nights. In the case of the embedded system at the startup, we had a lot of limitations in terms of the available memory and processing power on the device itself, as well as a lack of testing frameworks and tools; we have no such excuses as

SaaS owners. Memory, storage, and CPU cycles are cheap, and testing and monitoring frameworks are available in abundance.

Ideally, we've recognized these risks when constructing these systems, and shifted the focus left (earlier in the development process) as appropriate. Hardware and embedded system development has much stricter, more waterfall like development processes with substantially more rigorous pre-release testing than a mobile game due to the higher cost of errors appearing later in the software lifecycle for example.

We'll discuss some ways to shift left in more detail in the preventative measures section. Suffice it to say that your comprehensive serviceability plan is not a substitute for testing, and additionally doesn't excuse your development team from baking in reliability.

In the context of this book, we're considering the Serviceability of a SaaS system using an agile continuous delivery process. There are certain implied expectations with respect to high-availability, and the ability of the SaaS to adapt to market changes quickly by adding new features.

With this expectation of rapid iteration and high availability, we must recognize higher risk in terms of the shorter development cycle. Unlike aerospace or financial systems, which are highly regulated, and exhaustively tested and certified over the course of years, SaaS features are typically released on a bi-weekly or monthly basis. Irrespective of the thoroughness of our pre-deployment testing and peer reviews, we're much more likely in a continuous deployment SaaS environment to see bad code reach production, and touch the customer experience.

In addition to the risks we assume due to rapid iteration, there are also risks inherent in the complexity of modern SaaS systems. Distributed systems have evolved from simple systems such as single file servers with a thin veneer of a UI used to access some random CSV or some such, to monstrous polyglot systems spread across the globe.

Consider an example of a real system I've worked on: more than a half dozen dependent services, languages including Python, Java, C++, Bash, Go, JavaScript; build and deployment tools including Puppet, Chef, OpenStack, AWS, Docker, Tomcat, Express, Jenkins; persistence mechanisms including Riak, Ceph, Redis, Cassandra, Postgres, Kafka, Whisper, InfluxDB, ES; testing frameworks and tools including Jasmine, Junit, Sonar, Mockito; and numerous related serviceability tools. To top it all off, your client code can run in a number of different configurations: as a thick client from a desktop in any of the flavors of Linux, Windows, OSX; as a thick Mobile client on iOS or Android, and as a web client from that same pool of operating systems across a matrix of different web browsers, and even different versions of those web browsers. The client can also communicate with services in a number of different ways: UDP, WebSockets, IPC, REST, by passing messages to a queue, and so on; talk about bad big O complexity!

The middleware between all of these various interactions also needs to keep security in mind, and implement a layer to prevent malicious users from accessing and affecting the underlying services. After all, these endpoints, for the most part, are available to anyone that ping them.

This security layer involves various intermediary servers to check the validity and authenticity of certificates presented by clients, to parse and reject certain requests to avoid common cross site scripting and injection attacks, and to validate tokens and credentials with auth servers. These security considerations alone add a goodly dose of complexity to any SaaS.

I can't even count the number of times we've had customer reported issues because of various unintended interactions with cross site and script injection filters, or the number of times some ACL associated with a user account has been incorrectly configured granting too much or too little access to a given user (you mean you didn't want your intern to have the ability to execute "sudo rm -rf /"? Oops!).

Aside from the complexity of the implementation itself, the system is also spread across a multitude of servers in a variety of locations. In many cases this is done to allow servers closer to a customer's location to serve requests, thus making them more efficient. In some cases, this is done to comport to privacy laws in given countries. Duplicating the service may also be done simply because the sheer number of requests is difficult for single instances to handle.

In the EU for example, there are some draconian laws about how PII (publicly identifiable information) and other data must be handled and stored; essentially, you have to have servers in the EU if you want to do business there. So now your service has to consider both the origin and the destination of the requests when routing requests and retrieving and storing information.

In other cases, we're using an active-active set up. We have the services duplicated across various datacenters, and at any given time each DC is servicing some subset of these requests. In the event there is some failure in one of the locations, we can route traffic to one or more of the other datacenters while we triage the bad DC. We typically accomplish this with some sort of a proxy server layer that applies simple ratio routing in the happy path scenario, or applies other business rules to incoming requests based on the health of our backend servers. Such a setup increases the durability of the service and helps us increase our uptime.

Inherent in this distribution across servers, paradoxically, we also now assume risks with respect to network and availability issues due to configuration bugs. One of the difficult things about errors that occur at the proxy layer are they tend to not be associated with a robust logging framework and exception generating engine. You may see a hard 4XX HTTP return code emitted, but there is typically very little in the way of error logs for the sake of efficiency. The complexity of network topology itself can become a source of downtime and degraded service events as a result.

I recall working with a very complicated voice over IP system. The system interacted with several different cloud providers, as we did not have 100% of the necessary pieces of the puzzle in house. Some outside vendor help with some of the SIP trunk provisioning, another internal cloud handled the conversion of SIP to REST, and our service handled consuming the REST calls and returning results which went back through in the opposite direction.

When there was an issue in this complicated chain of interactions, it was a major production to track it down. The network topology itself was very complex, as we routed from PSTN (public switched telephony) networks to our external vendor, and then to our private cloud, which would itself interact with other distinct, different internal clouds. Each of these external and internal vendors had different approaches and opinions about the rigor and depth of what was required for Serviceability, and all had their own ticket and reporting systems.

Imagine having to debug low level SIP signaling across multiple clouds, having to file multiple internal tickets, and finally, having to file a ticket with an external vendor and babysit it all. Does that sound like a process that moves quickly, or easily?

Although the stories I've shared above probably resonant, and you're tearing up a little empathizing with poor old me, dollars to donuts, the customer was not feeling it. Customer expectations in an age of gigabit internet and smart phones that have thousands of times the processing power and memory they did just a decade ago are exceptionally high.

Customers expect four nines of uptime, and if you can't give it to them, there is someone else in the crowded SaaS marketplace that can (or will at least convince the customer they can). Additionally, customers don't judge a SaaS by uptime alone, they also expect things to be functionally correct as well (go figure).

Now, after examining, and understanding the nature of the risks we assume utilizing a continuous delivery paradigm to deliver SaaS systems, we can begin to shape what Serviceability is, and should do in this context.

We will have downtime and degraded service events due to network issues; we will have downtime and degraded experience events with respect to end user interactions. As SaaS owners, we accept that it is impractical, unreasonable, or impossible to prevent all breaking changes and unexpected, undesirable states all of the time; not to say we shouldn't try.

Serviceability in the context of a SaaS system means planning for the worst to happen, and minimizing the time we spend in downtime or degraded states.

Now, let's solidify our Serviceability goals as SaaS owners:

- Identify a bad state has happened

- Identify the source of the unexpected outcome

- Minimize the amount of time the system spends in a bad state

- Support the ability to deploy emergency changes

- Ultimately develop a permanent fix, and release the changes to resolve the issue permanently

In order to fulfill the goals with respect to Serviceability in a SaaS offering, we need several components.

Metrics: the ability of the system to emit meaningful, concise information about the internal state of the system in such a manner as to disambiguate the source of unexpected, undesired system states.

Monitoring: the ability to consume, understand, and visualize the metrics a system emits.

Alerting: the ability to inform the appropriate parties, as quickly as possible, based on the state of monitors, that undesired system states are eminent or ongoing.

Logging: the ability to associate the alerts and metrics we've received with the error messages and logs associated with the bad state.

A holistic framework, and a plan of action: a system of processes with respect to mitigating actions based on alerts

Learnings: post incident review and improvement of processes going forward.

These concepts will be discussed in detail in their respective chapters. However, we'll first discuss the policies and processes that can be put in place prior to deploying your code to mitigate the inherent risks associated with continuous delivery SaaS.

Preventative Measures

The overall goal and general scope of this book is to define and understand what Serviceability is in the context of a continuous delivery SaaS. So discussing preventative measures may seem a bit outside the scope of those stated goals; however, given common misunderstandings of what the role of Serviceability and its associated implementation should do, it is worth defining the role of the pre-deployment pipeline.

Although we just spent a goodly number of pages discussing and defining what Serviceability means in the context of a SaaS offering, it behooves us to flesh out the role of the earlier stages of the development and deployment process. Once we've defined the general roles of continuous delivery and integration pipelines, we can dovetail into the role of metrics.

Too often, without a solid understanding of the end to end lifecycle of the application development and deployment process, we have some gross misuse of metrics, monitors, and alerts. By defining our pre-deployment workflow, we can now defined what Serviceability is not.

Unit Testing

This may seem like a no-brainer to a lot of folks, but I've worked at places where unit testing was considered a time waster, because the developers always wrote flawless code. As you can imagine, we had a lot of fun debug sessions under the burning eyes of the boss due to this lackadaisical attitude.

Although the opinions on the merits of unit testing may vary from person to person, I can assure you the time spent writing unit tests is time well spent. In general, my philosophy has been to have a unit test for every branch, as well as all happy path and rainy day scenarios. I've occasionally made allowances for certain exceptions that were nearly impossible to mock due to the eccentricities of a given test framework, but as a general rule, cover it if you can.

Guidelines in terms of percentages vary, but at least 75% branch and 85% line coverage is a reasonable goal in my experience. Some zealots get obsessed with getting every last drop of coverage possible. Not only are these people incredibly frustrating to get peer reviews from ("Are you sure 1 + 1 is 2? You need to write a test for this!"), but writing that many unit tests can lead to an overall test suite that is incredibly brittle, and requires an unreasonable amount of effort to change and maintain.

At a high level, unit testing should capture the functionality of individual classes, and methods. We will not be placing metrics in the code to determine how long your method call took, or if it returned the expected value; that is not the goal of metrics for Serviceability, such concerns need to be addressed in unit testing.

Peer Review

Peer reviews are a great second step to the pre-deployment pipeline process when applied correctly. Having more seasoned engineers check code prevents painful lessons learned from repeating, and also helps develop the skills of less experienced engineers on the team.

No amount of testing can replace a good engineer combing over a piece of code, so peer reviews are an effective way to reduce the risks of breaking changes making it to production.

For example, there are cases where the wrong parameters are passed to a dependent service, or there may be some rate limiting concerns, etcetera.

Unfortunately, peer reviews are another tool that can be wielded by the dark side as well. I've worked with engineers that were convinced they were Dijkstra, Hopper, Torvalds, or Turing. No amount of convincing would sway them, and we'd end up in messy meetings with managers.

Don't be this person. Peer reviews should be used to find and fix bugs, performance concerns, and other general correctness issues; not to evangelize your particular opinions about just how modular code should be, or if a variable should be named Foo or Bar. Interview processes for tech companies are notoriously rigorous, so it is generally a safe bet your coworker is generally competent, and has a good reason for doing something the way they did.

Some rules that we adopted which were helpful: if you have a comment related to general correctness, and the comment is not addressed, you can block the commit from going into the pipeline; if you have a non-correctness comment, and the person does not agree with you, get second opinion, if the second opinion also does not agree, let it go.

In a fast moving continuous delivery model, we as developers and engineering managers don't have time to have religious arguments about things that are not about functional correctness. That said, peer reviews are an awesomely powerful way to prevent bad code from getting into production and causing issues.

Component Testing

This one may or may not apply to your particular project, but in many cases can be quite helpful. The goal of component testing is to test the coarser grained interactions with your service. On a backend service, this will entail interactions with APIs (usually RESTful).

Dependent services are replaced with mocks that return a given response when provided an expected input. Component testing confirms that if dependent services return their expected values, your service will function as expected.

Component tests are often used as a way to gate deployment into your pre-production environment. The thinking is that we can be good tenants of our cloud space by not pushing breaking changes into the collective pre-production testing environment.

It is always bothersome to be on-call, get paged due to a failure in your pre-production environment, and finding out it is because your dependent service did not have adequate component testing. You essentially end up doing their work for them, and you're almost without exception less familiar with their service than they are, so this is a big time waste for everyone.

Pre-production Environment

After you've successfully passed unit testing, peer reviews, and component testing, you still shouldn't be deploying to your production environment. Ideally, you have a pre-production environment that is essentially a smaller scale version of your production environment.

This can be an environment that is exercised by internal

developers, project managers, and other stake holders, as well as suites of automation and end to end tests. The general goal of the environment is to catch unexpected issues that are otherwise difficult to find using traditional testing methods and peer reviews.

Some of these issues include memory and thread leaks, deadlock and livelock, network issues, and unexpected usage patterns from users. These kinds of issues are notoriously difficult to catch with any kind of testing, so having a soak period, and allowing real people to try the service prior to deploying to the general public is always a good idea.

The amount of time you'll want to let your service soak is a matter of debate, but a good rule of thumb is at least a couple of days. My personal preference is to push about twice a week from pre-production to production. When pre-production soak starts to stretch out to a once a sprint event, you end up with many different changes queued up, and all deploying at once. Deploying multiple changes to production makes rolling back to previous versions messier with traditional code versioning systems, and makes it much more difficult to start to disambiguate the source of the issue.

If you're only deploying one or two changes at a time, you're typically able to quickly narrow down the source of the trouble. Additionally, it is much simpler to manually verify your changes in production when you only have to verify a couple of minor changes at a time; and you should always be manually verifying your changes in production!

The argument for less frequent deployments to production presumes the longer code is in the pre-production environment, the more likely we are to catch errors prior to pushing out to customers. In my experience, this is rarely the case; most defects can be caught rather quickly in pre-production, and the additional complexity of debugging problems associated with a jumble of changes in production is not worth the trade off.

End to End Tests

End to end tests are useful for finding defects once everything is deployed and talking to real services. While component tests verify the functionality of your service's APIs given the happy path scenario of all of your dependent services performing as expected, end to end tests verify that this is actually the case.

End to end tests can be integrated into the deployment pipeline such that they run immediately after a given version of your code is deployed. In the event of a failure in your pre-production environment, you can mark the version to prevent deployment to production, thus preventing bad code from reaching the end user. In the event of a failure in the production environment, you can quickly apply a hot fix, or roll back to the previous version if appropriate.

End to end tests prevent the scenario where your end user is finding issues and reporting them, or failure metrics start tripping pager alerts and waking up your engineers at 2AM; both the customer and your on-call engineers will appreciate them.

In most cases, you can reuse your end to end tests. That is, simple dependency injection of the pre-production and production service URLs as appropriate should allow the suites to be used in either environment (or however many pre-production layers you happen to have; I've worked at places that had 4 or 5).

Naturally, like unit tests, we're not aiming to cover 100% of every possible interaction with the user interface. Such a test suite would be extremely complex, brittle, and generally not too much fun to work with. We recognize that it is impractical to catch every potential error.

Things we don't expect to catch with end to end tests include things such as bugs with temporal or sequence causes, intermittent bugs such as rare race conditions, obscure browser compatibility issues, and inefficient queries or use cases. The general idea is to interact with most of the main touch points, and verify that expected results are returned.

While it may seem redundant to have end to end tests in pre-production as well as production, due to the ease of reusing most modern testing frameworks using dependency injection, the low cost of CPU cycles, and the not slim possibility of a delta between pre-production and production environments, it is worth it.

Load Tests

Load tests are simply frameworks which hit your service with incrementally higher request loads. Such frameworks might be as simple as a Bash script using cURL, or a sophisticated GUI driven affair which records page loads and so on. In any case, the general goal of such tests is the same: see what happens to a service when exposed to a varying volumes of different types of workloads.

Load testing serves several useful purposes. With respect to the effect of various loads on CPU capacity, free memory, and threads, we gain an understanding of how much traffic a given instance of our service can handle prior to experiencing resource exhaustion or other errors.

Such information can be used to give engineers baseline levels of performance, and aid in understanding when application behavior is abnormal. With this information in hand, engineers can make informed decisions about when it is necessary to trigger alerts and act on resource or error notifications.

In the context of an elastic service, information from load tests can also be used to inform automated instantiation of new instances. Spinning up new instances ensures that your QoS stays in line with your expectations.

Load tests should be run prior to launching any new service. Results are vital for designing appropriate monitoring and alerting, as well as getting a general idea about what to expect in the wild. There is some debate as to whether or not it is important to run load tests periodically. The thinking is we can catch application performance degrading based on recent changes, and take some sort of corrective action.

While well intentioned, having someone manually interpret load test results tends to be a waste of time in that a well instrumented system will already report request latency, and we can simply do a periodic review of our graphs to see if we're still achieving our desired QoS. Additionally, load tests have a tendency to trigger pages and alerts on our dependent services, waking up engineers at 2AM, and generally wasting time. For this reason, my general philosophy has been to only run load tests when first developing and deploying new applications or major features.

What Serviceability is Not

Now that we've touched on various pre-deployment sanity checks, and discussed what Serviceability is in the context of a SaaS system, we should have a good idea what Serviceability is not. Serviceability is not an excuse to be lax on testing, peer reviews, or generally being a good steward of your collective cloud space.

Leaning on the monitors and pages of an upstream service by neglecting your service's pre-deployment sanity checks and post-deployment testing is a surefire way to get on the bad side of your neighbor's engineering manager. Be a good neighbor, and do everything you can to avoid tripping an alarm and waking someone up at 2AM.

Serviceability is the last line of defense. Your metrics, monitors, alerts, and graphs are there for finding those head scratchers you couldn't have reasonably been expected to find in during the pre-deployment process.

Metrics

Metrics is an overloaded term in the context of computer science and enterprise software systems. From a project owner perspective, the general understanding of metrics is one of usage and behavior. That is, business stakeholders tend to view metrics in the context of how much usage a given feature is receiving, how many "get help" requests were made, how many customers from a given country are logging in; metrics for the purpose of analysis of customer behavior and billing purposes.

From an engineering and Serviceability perspective, metrics refer to the general behavior of the service with respect to QoS and correctness of responses. While some serviceability metrics may also double as general business metrics, such as total call volume, we are not aiming to please the insatiable appetite of project owners for customer usage and behavior metrics.

In fact, we aim to keep these two worlds as far apart as possible. On the non-engineering side of things, I've found that project owners assume QoS and Serviceability. It is therefore important to be able to present cogent metric driven arguments to justify placing feature development on hold if Serviceability and QoS metrics are not up to snuff.

Customer behavior and usage metrics should never be driving project priorities towards feature development at the expense of QoS or Serviceability. On the contrary, application stability and QoS need to be the paramount concern of not only the engineering personnel, but also project owners.

Unarguably, a SaaS lives and dies by its reputation for reliability. A customer might be a bit annoyed that they can't use the latest and greatest widget on your SaaS, but would be willing to wait a little while for it, and is extremely unlikely to drop your product all together due to some trivial feature being missing. A customer is much less tolerant of seeing "Service Unavailable" or a never-ending loading icon, will post about their issues on social media, potentially sue your company, and definitely take their business elsewhere.

Good Serviceability metrics are part of our overall framework that acts as a warning of impending failures, and an alarm bell for ongoing issues. They are vital for preventing the system from going offline entirely, as well as for minimizing our mean time to recovery.

While we touched on some things we will not be placing metrics on in the preventative measures section, we'll expand here in depth and breadth. Metrics should be designed and implemented such as to be a sufficiently coarse grained expression of application state and behavior, while still be unambiguous enough to be meaningful to on-call engineers.

For example, we don't want to include the class name and line number a failure originated from in a metric being emitted; that is far too specific, and such specificity is best left to other more appropriate tools such as loggers (more on that later). Conversely, we don't want metrics that are simple reflections of system state represented by stoplight colors - e.g.: "Your system state is Red!" - as those metrics are too ambiguous, and force the on-call engineer to do a lot of investigation prior to even beginning to address the cause.

Serviceability metrics are the bridge between the application state and the monitoring framework that will alert on-call engineers. Think of Serviceability metrics as the compiler that converts the system state into a slightly more meaningful expression. While they don't need to be so informative that an engineer can make a snap decision about the cause of a bad system state, they do need to be easy enough to understand quickly in an emergency situation.

Where to Put Metrics

While it might seem clever to have every single method, class, and general sneeze of your application sending metrics, such an approach gets unwieldy very quickly. There are several reasons: if you have layer upon layer of metrics, you can subsequently receive multiple alerts for the same issue; maintaining an understandable plan of action for such a complicated collection of metrics is difficult and time consuming, and sending an exorbitant amount of metrics can impact application performance, as such transactions are not free in terms of bandwidth, CPU, memory, and thread usage.

Additionally, the causes of failures in a distributed system with a rigorous set of pre-deployment sanity checks tend to be reasonably limited, so such intricate and numerous metric emissions from the application are not strictly necessary to achieve our Serviceability goals. In general, in a declarative program, given good input, you can expect a certain output. Taking this a step further, if your declarative program is supplying proper input to another service, you can reasonably assume an expected response. As such, the main areas of failure in a SaaS will be ingress and egress points of the service.

Thus, we've now reductively arrived at our problem areas: input from clients of our service, and by extension, requests from our service to other services. Hence, we need to have coarse grained metrics around our SaaS' APIs, as well as any interaction of our SaaS with another service.

There is one other category of metrics we require, most especially on a back-end service; resource metrics. As discussed in the load test section, we need to be aware of how much free memory, CPU capacity, and free threads we have, as well as the frequency of garbage collection. Services running on instances with low resources may be intolerably slow in serving requests, resulting in request timeouts and failures.

Deadlock and livelock issues can occupy all threads on a SaaS instance, and the application layer will have no way to express this meaningfully without resource metrics. In extreme cases, out of memory exceptions may also be seen, and these get tricky to debug if you're not instrumenting correctly, as instances without memory are most probably not sending anything to the log server. Naturally, these metrics won't apply to client side applications not running on our enterprise servers.

What to Send Metrics About

Expanding on the earlier reductive reasoning in terms of where to put metrics, we can similarly express the general cases of failures in our application. I expanded a bit on some special cases in regards to resource metrics, but in the general case, requests into, and from our service fail in two modes: hard failure such as HTTP 401, 403, 500, 502, 503; and due to a service not responding to a request within the application's required or expected time frame.

So then, reductively, we have failures due to latency, and other failures due to hard system states. Combining with our earlier reduction, we can derive our application's metrics requirements: latency and failure metrics for ingress points (our APIs), and our egress points (our calls to another service's APIs).

While the subset of metrics a SaaS should emit is relatively straightforward, there is a lot of additional scaffolding, documentation, and policy to consider; we'll discuss that next. First, though, we'll need to discuss code organization in order to set the stage for how to integrate metrics with an overall Serviceability framework and plan of action.

Code Organization for Serviceability in SaaS

While I won't suppose I've found an infallible truth with respect to code organization, in the context of Serviceability, I have found some general conventions which aid in creating meaningful metrics. Based on our early reductive reasoning, we've arrived at the conclusion that our ingress and egress points should be the source of our serviceability metrics. Thus, those pieces of our code, logically, fall under the purview of Serviceability.

Isolating interactions with dependent services - services upon which our service relies to perform its stated function - to modular clients can greatly reduce code duplication, and ensure consistency in the application of metric names. This is vitally important for the proper functionality of monitors which will consume these metrics. I've seen cases where metric names were misspelled in one place or another, and as a result, the monitors we created to alert us of failures were not able to notice bad system states.

Along with the use of modular clients for calls to external services, the use of a constants file is also quite helpful. The use of named constants rather than inline text comes naturally to many developers, but I have seen a great many of otherwise very talented developers simply throw some double quotes around a metric name and call it good. This can lead to the same naming errors discussed earlier, and make our monitors blind to failures as a result. Using the convention that all metric names should come from a shared constants file prevents such misspellings from happening.

As much as possible, our ingress points should reflect their associated API names. For example, on a backend service with an addressable REST endpoint of "/api/v1/customerecord/{Record ID}" using a GET verb, we might name our main associated API method "getCustomerRecord". Similarly, on a client application or module, we should aim to name our call to an external service in such a manner that the underlying API we're interacting with is clear at a glance.

The general principal behind using common method names and API entry point names is one of efficiency. Having closely associated API and method names can allow monitors to directly consume metrics, and send alerts that inform on-call engineers what specific ingress or egress point is failing. Such conveniences, when taken with other measures we'll discuss later, can add up to substantial time savings. Even minutes of downtime events can have devastating impacts at scale. We definitely felt the pressure every single second a customer was not able to register a sale when I worked at the world's largest e-commerce site, as at that scale, each minute represented thousands of requests to our service.

Additionally, avoid the trap of having fun with naming your SaaS and your SaaS' methods. As an on-call engineer having to figure out why you named your named your SaaS after an anime character, or why your metric name is your favorite

Greek god is not a productive use of my time.

Your API metrics should do as much as possible to disambiguate the source of an issue; remember every minute your on-call has to spend figuring out what is generating an error is another minute the customer is experiencing frustrating interactions with your money making machine: the SaaS pays your salary, so code accordingly.

Naming Conventions

As discussed in the previous section, as much as possible, your metrics should be meaningfully named. Further, your metrics names should be related to the associated API ingress or egress point, and the HTTP verb if applicable, or other meaningful verb-like-thing if you are interacting with the API via an SDK that abstracts the return code of whatever service(s) it is interacting with.

Expanding a bit, if you have an API which supports multiple action verbs, a good, quick, and useful thing to do is simply prepend the method name with the verb: getCustomerRecord, postCustomerRecord, putCustomerRecord, deleteCustomerRecord, and so on.

We've now defined the base for our metric naming schema, but there is still some work to do. As discussed, most modern SaaS are multi-regional, multi-instance, multi-role creatures. As such, we may want or need to create monitors that differ depending on such conditions, for example, I may want to set the alerts for my EU instances to different thresholds, or to send the metrics to different parties due to the eccentricities of data privacy laws there. Similarly, I may want to distinguish between my pre-production and production environment's metrics without setting up different metrics brokers.

Using dependency injection, we can set the values of configurable variables to prepend to our metric base prior to sending to our metrics collection services. By always adopting this practice, even prior to having a specific need for it, we are future proofing our implementation; that is we are preparing to be a multi-region, multi-dc, multi-environment SaaS. The effort involved to dynamically prepend a metric name using dependency injection is pretty small for a modern SaaS given that any sufficiently advanced and ambitious service is already using some manner of dependency injection.

We've now defined our prefix, and our base metric name. Next comes the task of categorizing and reporting our postfix. The postfix of the metric name details what particular bucket this metric falls in, or if the metric is the agnostic latency kind. While it is tempting to get fancy with your postfix codes, in my experience, a general bucketing approach works fine.

In the case of very fine grained postfix values, we would have a unique post fix for every possible return code. For example, USA.Prod1.getCustomerRecord.401, USA.Prod1.getCustomerRecord.200, and so on. The issue in this case is the prospect of consuming these metrics in your monitors, setting appropriate thresholds, and subsequently sending an alert to your on-call engineers.

Given that response codes in the rainy day scenario can be a mixed bag, we can receive a very small pool of several kinds of errors, and accidentally miss being informed by our monitors. Consider getting a peppering of 401, 403, and 404 HTTP return codes among a majority of 200s. Unless you have an obscenely sensitive monitor, you may miss these errors. You could aggregate all of the 4XX errors into a single bucket on the monitoring end of things if your framework allows it, but such calculations would undoubtedly be resource intensive relative to bucketing on the application side. Additionally, in my experience, monitoring tools are relatively immature, prone to having issues in complex use cases, and generally difficult to work with.

Rather than attempting to aggregate on the monitor side of things, we can use a combination of bucketing, and adequate logging of exceptions and errors on the application side of things. The code you've written your application in is undoubtedly more mature and apt at aggregating than any monitoring framework I've worked with, so do it there.

Using the general taxonomy of your underlying ingress and egress points, you can easily conceive of buckets. In the case of SDKs, this might be as simple as a "Success" and "Fail" post fix, as the client application is often unaware of the specifics of the internal workings of the SDK's interaction with a given API. In the case of HTTP status codes, general leading digit bucketing works in my experience. Something like 2XX = "Success", 4XX = "Error" or "ClientSideError", and 5XX = "Fail" or "ServerSideFailure".

Thusly, we can bucket our metrics into one of a few states for the purposes of monitors and alerts. If you're really dead-set on knowing exactly how many 401s versus 404s, you can easily enough exclude or include one or another in a given bucket by implementing a check in the code (e.g.: if (httpStatus == 404){ postFix = 404} else { postFix = "Error"}). Alternatively, you could also send two metrics, one fine grained metric, and one bucketed metric.

In my opinion and experience, however, such fine grained metric postfixes do not do much to disambiguate causes, the on-call still has to follow the same troubleshooting steps involving grepping logs, and such fine grained postfixes also add complexity to the implementation of monitors which tend to be less mature and less amenable to the needs of the modern SaaS developer. Additionally, the documentation end of things, especially in the case of runbooks, can get a little convoluted as a result.

If your metrics and monitoring frameworks support it, you may find it useful to add a tracking ID as one of the components of the naming convention as well. If such an addition will not complicate the prospect of generating graphs using your chosen solution, and also will not interfere with your monitoring and alerting, you can sometimes short-circuit the search for a specific failed API call. That is, if you're able to get a UUID that isolates a failure based on very concise metric data, you may save some time versus grepping logs or throwing Lucene queries at things.

This additional field is strictly optional, as your backend services need to have good enough Serviceability that a UUID is not strictly necessary to begin to track down an issue. I'll discuss the relationship between metrics, tracking information, and logging as they relate to the overall Serviceability framework later in the book. For now, it is sufficient to state a backend service should somehow be mapping the log messages to the naming schema used to describe the API interactions, should always be logging every exception, and should always be logging enough meta-data about any failed call such that any request to the API should be discoverable and debuggable with or without an initial tracking ID. Additionally, there should always be some unique identifier in the logs associated with an individual request, whether or not the requester initially sent one in order to support the isolation of a single discrete interaction with a given service or set of services.

Being able to quickly grep logs or a set of metrics, and find a unique identifier that will allow you track an instance of a failed API call is essential. The manner in which this is accomplished can vary however. If you choose to generate the unique identifier on the end user's client (web client, thick client, etc.), and pass this to the backend services, you can insert this value in the metric name; again, only if this is appropriate for your specific framework, and will not complicate generating meaningful graphs, monitors, and alerts (more on those later).

A tracking ID should be a UUID, and should be generated on a per request basis. Once generated, simply insert into a predetermined location in your metric name. For example "USA.Prod1.{UUID}.getCustomerRecord.401", or any other similar positioning that will not interfere with the ability of your on-call to generate the necessary graphs, monitors, and alerts.

The tracking ID is nice to have in the metric name, but is not essential. The primary role of metrics is to express the state of the system in such a way that other tools can consume that state, and engineers can be aware of impending or ongoing bad system states as a result.

The role of metrics, strictly speaking, is not to inform about the specifics of a failure. Code should be generally organized such that metric names that represent their state should be self documenting to some degree, and postfix codes should also aid in disambiguating the source of a bad system state so as to reduce the search space, and reduce mean time to recovery. The role of providing more detailed, specific information, however, is best delegated to logging tools, which are much more well suited to be expressive enough to aid in debugging. That said, provided we do not go too deep down the rabbit hole, a simple UUID in the metric name can aid in debugging.

Allow me to expand a bit on what I mean by going too far down the rabbit hole. I've seen attempts to conflate the roles of logs and metrics. That is, there is an attempt to use metrics as a substitute for logging on the server side applications and the network layers between the client and the server. For example, a metric named

"USA.Prod1.{UUID}.{CUSTOMER_ID}.{CUSTOMER_ACTI ON}.{ERROR_MESSAGE}.{CLIENT_TYPE}.{OPERATING _SYSTEM}.{CUSTOMER_TYPE}.getCustomerRecord.401"

This is a fool's errand: no matter how many postfixes, prefixes, tweaks, and tricks you try with your metric, you will never completely replace the functionality of logs and events.

Once we've accepted that metrics cannot supplant the role of logs and events entirely, we can start to realize we've been trying to use a hammer on a screw.

The prospect of populating all of the fields in our monstrous "rabbit hole" metric is a daunting one. If we're using an aspect oriented framework, we somehow have to propagate all of that information to the interceptor. If we're not using an AOP framework, we need to pass all of this information around from method to method in order to keep track of it until we finally emit our metric. In either case, this is a clunky, ugly, and messy proposition. With a logging solution, we can simply use the metadata store of the thread, and stamp every entry with whatever metadata your little heart desires, or log the metadata as soon as we receive it in the case of errors: no fuss, no muss.

Since we cannot replace logs, we may as well not further complicate the code which is used to generate metrics in an effort to do so. Use the right tool for the right job; metrics are thin abstractions of state consumed by monitors, which are used to generate alerts, which in turn get the attention of on-call engineers who then do a deep-dive using highly detailed and expressive logging tools (Apache server logs, Kibana using Lucene queries, Splunk etc.) to diagnose the exact cause of a failure.

Logging frameworks are well suited to generate dynamic views based on whatever particular request metadata you are interested in. It is relatively simple to distill the noise of the log cluster down to the precise expression you are looking for on the fly, whereas it is virtually impossible to think of all of the use cases you might have for request metadata ahead of time when creating your metrics schema.

The use of metrics and logs are not mutually exclusive, on the contrary, one is very difficult to derive value from without the other. There is no reason we cannot emit a concise log entry with exception and error information as well as request metadata alongside our metric; our SaaS can and should be emitting metrics as well as meaningful, concise, organized log data. I'll expand on logging and such in more depth later.

We've discussed naming conventions at length, and undoubtedly, there are some readers shaking their heads because they are locked into some legacy framework that will not give them the kind of flexibility needed to implement any of the suggestions. Fear not poor soul, we'll discuss some solutions to having poorly named metrics in the documentation section. For now, just implement as closely as you can using one of the suggested approaches, and double down on the documentation side of things.

Metric Documentation

Although we've done our best to name our metrics in a meaningful way that disambiguates the source and informs an on-call engineer where to start looking, there is more we can do. Ideally an engineer can quickly become familiar with a naming schema, and know how to grep code to locate the source. However, on large projects, projects with teams at multiple sites and time zones, often times changes can be introduced that not every team member is aware of. Additionally, engineers that are new to teams, or engineers from other teams that want to interpret your graphs, and may not have the basis to understand the meaning of your metrics are potential use cases to consider.

As a general policy, metrics should follow some agreed upon naming convention for their prefix, base, and post fix. Even an imperfect naming schema is better than ad-hoc chaos, so pick your poison and document it.

How in-depth you should go with respect to documentation is a matter of debate, but minimally, you should have a basic mapping. Consider the documentation to be a hash table designed for Big O(1) lookups by the on-call engineer.

Given that not every on-call engineer is cognizant of every new change, we need to do all we can to aid in their expedient understanding of the source of an alert. To that end, you and your team(s) should maintain a simple table on some mutually accessible resource such as an internal wiki. The left hand column should be the metric name, the center column the general meaning, and the right hand column the API(s) interacted with. It is okay to bundle the various verbs if the meaning is the same, and a single central legend for prefixes is okay as well.

Postfix code	Meaning
Error	4XX HTTP return code
Fail	5XX HTTP return code
Success	2XX HTTP return code

Metric Name	Usage	Associated API
getCustRecord putCustRecord deleteCustRecord	Read, update, or delete of customer record from database	ourService/api/v1/CustRecord/{Record ID}
postCustRecord	Create customer record in database	ourService/api/v1/CustRecord

Feature Completion Guidelines for Metrics

After you've solidified this agreement with your team(s), also begin the process of formalizing requirements for accepting features as being completed. It would be great if we didn't have to have these sorts of formal reviews, but due to the fast moving nature of SaaS continuous delivery, the absence of extended testing cycles, and other complexities inherent to SaaS generally, it is vital we ensure we have all Serviceability metrics in place.

As part of the general sanity check prior to introducing a feature, even to pre-production, your team needs hard and fast rules that no new API level features, or new interactions with external services can be promoted without adequate metrics. There is no good way we can know if a new feature or interaction is failing in the wild if we don't have metrics around it after all.

Such a requirement need not be an onerous process. Using a straightforward aspect oriented framework you can easily isolate the changes needed to add new metrics to a 2 or 3 code line change in a couple of files. The first would be a change to the constants file we discussed earlier to add your new metric name, and the second to the outer wrapper that acts as the interceptor for your method calls. In our case, we were able to simply use a regular expression to capture all of the desired method calls. Since we had adopted the verb prefix naming convention for our main ingress and egress methods, all we had to do was annotate our new method, and voila, we had metrics.

Although aspect oriented programming has its limitations, such as some difficulties with instrumenting nested decorators in some implementations, some manner is available in most common programming languages, both 3rd and 4th generation. Additionally, well constructed metrics clients will allow for easy one offs if aspect oriented metrics are not an option for you, or if you have a special case. Sending a metric in a "finally" block rather than using an aspect decorator is not the end of the world, and it is not too much to ask of your team.

Metric Storage

Storage costs in general are one of the major expenses of your SaaS. As such, it is generally frowned upon to ask to indefinitely store your metric values. While well designed and named metrics are as narrow in scope as possible, and their names also similarly frugal in terms of length, a large enterprise scale SaaS can generate an enormous number of metrics in a very small amount of time.

While it is nice to have historical trends available in infinite permutations, for the purposes of Serviceability it is not strictly necessary. Sure there are some cool ML algorithms you could run on historical metrics data, and make some freaky accurate predictions about an impending bad system state, but barring something neato like that, you don't really need live metrics much beyond a couple of weeks. The majority of rule violations that trigger alerts via your monitors will have causes in the very near term; there is typically a close temporal relationship between the epicenter of the incident and the alert. As such, we typically don't need to go too far back in the past in our visualization tools to find the exact time and date where an abnormal trend first began.

However, for the sake of generating reports on longer term QoS and call traffic for the purposes of prioritizing performance work or making other architectural decisions relating to scaling up, we may occasionally want to take a look at the long view. One simple way of doing something like this is via decimation.

If we consider the line graph representation of the system's health and resource metrics to be a sort of analog representation of the internal state, we can apply a signal processing technique to them. Continuous analog signals are converted to discrete digital representations of themselves via a process known as sampling. That is, because digital equipment by the nature of its binary logic cannot truly represent an analog signal wave, we instead take a series of discrete measurements of the amplitude of the wave at a static rate. Then when converting these records from digital back into analog signals, we apply a trigonometric equation which is able to transform the digital samples of the analog signal back to a close facsimile of its continuous wave form. Well, that is if you ignore the sage advice of all your friends that insist on listening to analog vinyl records rather than iTunes, because they are really bothered by the loss of fidelity.

Using the signal wave analogy (pun intended), we can then apply decimation. Periodically, we can aggregate a given collection of measurements for a coarser grained time interval. That is, we can take a number of measurements and meta-measurements, and take the average value. This will become the new value for the given time interval. That is several minutes or more of the graph are condensed to a single data point, a single record.

We can then take these coarser grained measurements, and reconstruct a general representation of the initial signal, albeit with less fidelity. We don't have the same ability to look at peaks and values at the sub-minute interval, as we would need on occasion for the sake of Serviceability, but we do still have a decent idea what happened at a given data point a month ago. Signal decimation can save storage costs if you have a use case to look at longer term trends of serviceability metrics.

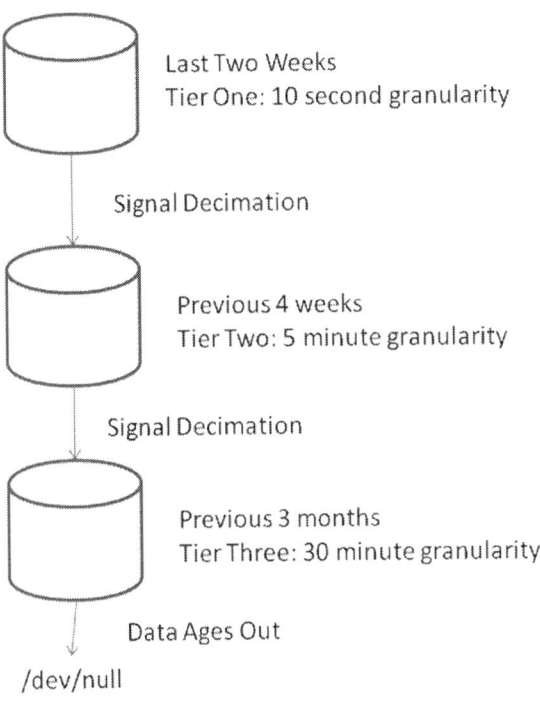

Last Two Weeks
Tier One: 10 second granularity

Signal Decimation

Previous 4 weeks
Tier Two: 5 minute granularity

Signal Decimation

Previous 3 months
Tier Three: 30 minute granularity

Data Ages Out

/dev/null

Monitors and Monitoring

Now that we've implemented a metrics framework in our code, adopted a prefix, base, and postfix naming schema; agreed on a standard for documentation, and also created a policy on where and when metrics need to be added, we can move on to the next component of our overall SaaS Serviceability framework: monitors.

Monitor is another overloaded term in computer science generally, so I'll take a paragraph or two to disambiguate. In the context of lower-level terminology a monitor is used to handle mutual exclusion with respect to the access of certain resources by competing threads. In the context of Serviceability, monitor is both a verb and a noun. As a verb, "monitoring" refers to the act of an engineer observing the state of an application by examining a visual or textual representation of the internal system state. Most commonly , this involves a grep of server logs, creation of Lucene or Splunk queries, and general eye-balling of line graphs with an X axis representing time, and a Y axis representing some level of a given metric representing an internal system state.

As a noun, in the context of SaaS Serviceability, a monitor is some manner of software tool that consumes metrics emitted by a SaaS system, and converts them into a representation of the system state. After converting the metrics into a representation of the internal system state, a monitor then applies static or dynamic rules on that system state via the use of alerts, and subsequent notifications are sent to a tool which informs appropriate personnel to take actions to address impending or ongoing bad system states.

Purpose of Monitors

The purpose of monitors is to take all the hard work you've done previously in implementing a metrics framework, consume the resulting output of the application, and apply intelligence to the results in order to make sure that no bad system states go unnoticed. Conceptually, the purpose of monitors is unambiguous, however, I've seen efforts to conflate metrics, monitors, and logs in such a way as to collapse the purposes of one or another into a sort of medley that plays multiple roles.

While the idea of collapsing the number of layers of your Serviceability framework may on its face seem to reduce complexity, in my experience such desires stem from a general lack of understanding of the entire holistic approach to Serviceability. From a business perspective, project and engineering managers are always eager to decrease the number of tools used to reduce the amount of code written, which theoretically speeds up the development process; and there is always an effort to reduce the number of licensing fees the development team needs to pay, so logically, it makes sense from a business perspective to conflate and collapse the metrics and Serviceability layers.

There are a number of products that are eager to fill this request by being an all in one plug-and-play tool that gets you "doing metrics" right out of the box with a simple one step installation process. As an experienced on-call engineer, these pitches always strike me like those get rich quick infomercials they play in the wee hours of the morning on unused television airtime. While appealing on its face, every single such implementation I have seen has failed in key areas; any gains you may make in terms of licensing fee savings, or development time reduction are easily eaten up by increased mean time to recovery from bad system states and damage to the reputation of the reliability of your product.

As discussed in the introductory chapter, modern SaaS systems are inherently complex, and thus their associated monitoring and alerting frameworks, naturally, will unavoidably be at least some related order of magnitude as complex. My general advice would be to view any all-in-one metrics and Serviceability solution with the same skepticism you would a snake oil salesman.

Additionally, it is vitally important to consider the impact that an insufficiently mature monitoring solution can have on your team. Consider, carefully and thoughtfully, that your monitors have the potential to cause someone to interrupt a dinner with a loved one, send an alert while someone is in the middle of a commute, in the shower, or sound asleep in the middle of the night. Poorly implemented monitors and alerts can lead to unhappy engineers, and unhappy engineers can lead to a revolving door of on-boarding new engineers because you've lost your more experienced engineers to a competitor.

Perpetual turnover due to incorrectly implemented Serviceability and alerting solutions is a vicious cycle. On a productivity front, your velocity suffers greatly; firstly because your more experienced and efficient engineers leave, secondly because your remaining engineers have to divide their time between ramping up new engineers and their normal duties, and thirdly because you now have less experienced engineers taking on daily responsibilities.

At this stage, invariably, there comes pressure from project managers and other stakeholders to maintain velocity. This can lead to engineers cutting corners to make more hours out of the day, working even longer hours, and becoming increasingly unhappy. As a result of cutting corners, technical debt accumulates, and the number of pages waking people up in the middle of the night increases. This in turn leads to more turnover, and the issue gets worse and worse.

I've been on teams that inherited these sorts of situations, and it took under 2 years for us to lose 40% of our engineers; not fun.

While my general goal was to avoid this book becoming cut-and-paste code, or a general collection of low-level implementation details, I will give some general advice about good open source tools you can use to implement your monitoring and alerting framework towards the end of the book. Managers will love them because they are free, and your engineers will love them because they are open source and have an active community of users.

Monitors are the last layer of the our SaaS Serviceability stack (although they share this layer with visualization tools which will be discussed later), and act as the bridge between the metrics the application emits and the on-call engineer's pager. Approach the idea of a monitor, and the subsequent choosing of an appropriate monitoring implementation with the general understanding of the goals of a monitor. To that end, we'll now discuss what a monitor needs to be able to do.

What a Monitor Needs to be Able to Do

The role of the monitor, and its subsequent necessities in terms of functionality, are naturally associated with the metrics emitted by your application. Thankfully, based on earlier chapters, you've implemented a framework that reduces the breadth and depth of the metrics the application emits using bucketing, and have appropriately delegated more detailed information emissions to logging frameworks (more on that later). As such, ideally, we will not have an unwieldy jumble of monitors that confound our sleepy on-call engineer that has been woken up at 2AM by an application failure page.

In a very general sense, a monitor needs to be able to convert raw metric data into a representation of the system state. To this end, your monitoring framework needs to have some manner of interface for persisting general rule sets with respect to when to send system alerts.

Much like your general metrics naming schema, your monitor needs to express violations of underlying rules in a meaningful manner. After all, we've gone to great lengths to make our metrics easy to understand in order to help our on-call engineers reduce mean time to recovery. Ideally, the monitoring framework should be able to do minimal work, and essentially express the ratios of metrics which caused a rule violation. Given that we have named our metrics meaningfully, these alerts triggered by rules violations should be self documenting in some sense.

Though we expect that monitors are essentially a pass through for metrics, and should be generally self documenting, we still expect and require that documentation exists as to what specifically these monitors mean. We'll discuss this more in the "Alerting" section of the book.

Beyond the core functionality, that is the ability to convert the metrics into a representation of the system state, and the ability create rules on which to determine if an on-call engineer needs to be informed on the basis of that system state; there are some nice-to-haves: regular expression support for rules, alarm suppression, alarm dependency chaining, and automated service ticket creation.

Regular expression support for rules is an awesome thing to have. I've worked with monitoring and alerting frameworks that had regular expression support, as well as with monitoring frameworks that did not have regular expression support. In the case of monitoring frameworks without regular expression support, each API in each datacenter, in each environment, for each postfix condition had to have its own rule and monitor. That is "US-1.getFoo.fail", "US-2.getFoo.fail", "US-1.getFoo.error", "US-2.getFoo.error", "CA-1.getFoo.fail", "CA-2.getFoo.fail", "CA-1.getFoo.error", "CA-2.getFoo.error" all had to have unique rule sets and monitors. Every time we added a new availability zone, renamed a datacenter, or changed a postfix value, we had to go through and rewrite, test, and verify every single rule on every single associated monitor.

Contrast this with the ease of a monitoring framework that supports regular expressions for rules. In the case of the "getFoo" example above, I could simply write a rule that stated:

*"apply rule A to ' * getFoo(\.fail|\.error)'"*

and I was done. Whenever we added a new datacenter, availability zone, or changed a postfix value, I would either have to do no work, or simply add a logical NOT or AND. At scale, these sorts of time savings start to add up.

Alarm suppression refers to the ability of the monitoring and alerting tool to support a manual override of an ongoing alert. Alarm suppression is useful in a number of situations. Alarm suppression can be used to silence alarms when there is planned system maintenance and a given service will be in a degraded or unavailable state. In such a case, you can avoid paging people out of bed, or the rigmarole of temporarily manually disabling monitors and alerts.

There are some other times when you might want to suppress alarms, such as during times of low total call volume, or when a given action will necessarily cause a degraded service state. During these states, we would like to have the ability for our rules to only be conditionally applied, because we are either aware of the cause of the degraded system state, or the application of the rule would result in an alert that did not indicate a real degraded or downtime event.

I recall on one occasion we had introduced a new SaaS service to a country that represented an emerging market for us, and adoption rates were exceptionally low at this early stage. As a result of this low usage pattern, we had very low total call volume. Due to the fact that we had low total call volume, whenever we had even a single error, it represented an enormous ratio of our overall calls, and would send an alert that would page an on-call engineer out of bed; not good.

The solution in this case was to apply a sort of "meta-rule" that is, a rule about our rule. We added an additional layer of filters to the rule. The additional layer of filters on the rule allowed us to only conditionally apply the rule if the total call traffic was over a certain threshold, and the failures therefore could be proven to be statistically significant. In the event the alert for this particular monitor in this particular country went off, we did a basic query on total call volume to the given API, and only if the value was greater than a given static value did we send out our alert. This cut down on bogus alerts, and helped us focus our development time on addressing real issues.

On other occasions, I've worked with services that maintained caches on the service side to avoid making expensive queries to our legacy database system. Naturally, a warmed up cache is much, much faster than making a query to a database for view configuration or other application data. So it stands to reason that when the application is redeployed as part of the standard continuous delivery process that at least initially requests will be slower on average from a cold, empty application side cache.

What would tend to happen with our SaaS components that relied on service side caches would be that clusters of queries on newly deployed instances of the service would be relatively slow. This relative slowness would in turn trip our latency rules, and this would subsequently page our on-call engineers en-masse as every single API on the service would experience the same relative latency issues.

The solution in this case was to simply suppress the latency monitors. By suppressing the alerts for the APIs of the service slightly prior to the deployment, and for fifteen or so minutes after, we completely avoided unnecessary pages. The alternative in this case had we not had the ability to suppress alerts would to have been to have much laxer latency rules with respect to alerts; not optimal.

Alarm dependency chaining comes in very handy for larger scale, more complex SaaS utilizing a micro service architecture. In the case of a complex modern SaaS, there are deep dependency chains. That is when service A calls service B, service B may in turn call service C, and also make queries to data store D. In such a situation, in the event that data store D is offline, or service C is in a bad state, any calls from service A to service B will fail, and if there are rules associated with the interaction, an alert will fire, and an on-call engineer will be paged.

In the worst case scenario in the aforementioned theoretical interaction, it is possible that on-call engineers from data store D team, service B team, as well as service A team will be paged. In the event that service B has multiple clients, we could see additional alerts being sent. In essence, we would have something on the order of, minimally, a half dozen engineers paged for what is really an issue with a single team's data store.

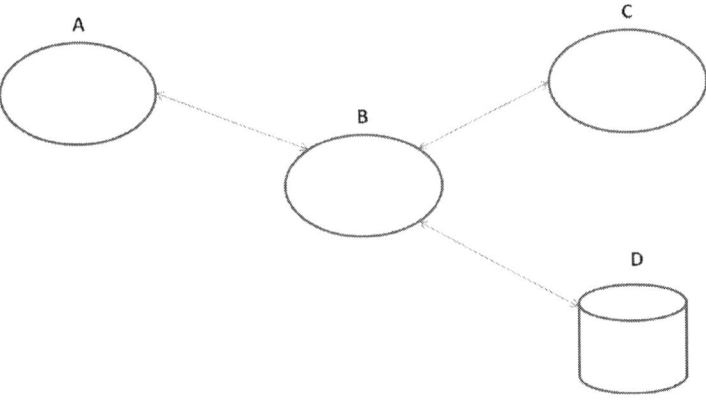

If this incident happens in the wee hours of the morning, you're waking up a half dozen folks that have likely already put in a typical 10-12 hour engineer day. They wake up, turn on the computer, try to shake off their sleepy brain, and start to investigate. After about 15 minutes, they figure out that the owners of data store D are already on the case, and they were woken up for no reason; frustrating. The engineer ACKs the page, explains the issue in the notes, and heads back to bed, only to be paged again an hour later, because data store

D is still down. Lather, rinse, repeat, and maybe start thinking about polishing that resume and applying somewhere that will let them get a little sleep.

Even if these sorts of incidents happen during business hours, and you are not waking an engineer up, you are wasting cycles. If an on-call engineer is periodically interrupted because of failures in services that they have no control over, you're wasting valuable development time. Additionally, as an on-call engineer that has been in this position, I can say, it is also stressful to have to explain at the end of the week why you weren't able to complete a given task due to the time you had to spend dealing with issues that had nothing to do with the service you are tasked with being responsible for; don't put your engineers in this position.

The solution here is the ability of the monitoring framework to associate a given alert with a set of filters that can reach across services. That is, the monitoring framework should support the ability to say:

if (dataStoreD Alert = true OR serviceB.Foo Alert = true) suppress alarm; else alert serviceA on-call

All the earlier work we did adopting a naming convention and documenting our schema starts to come in handy now, as engineers on other teams can visit our wikis and decide how to craft their suppression rules based on the names we've used for metrics; we've create an entire ecosystem! We'll discuss this more in the overall framework section.

Last on the list of nice to haves is automated service ticket creation. The monitoring framework itself doesn't necessarily need to directly support this, but needs to be amenable to feeding its info through a filtering script in such a manner as to allow access to its metadata in a way that enables us to create a mechanism that interacts with our service ticket system. The general principle with automated service ticket creation is one of enforcing the responsibility of a given application team to investigate all abnormal system states that result in a monitor's alert being fired.

In an ideal case, we have context information automatically populated in the ticket itself. For example, we'd include the time the alert was triggered, links to relevant graphs and log dashboards pre-set to the given time frame, and any other relevant metadata the monitoring framework has available.

I've worked in environments at smaller scale companies that had no real ticketing system to speak of, and this worked reasonably in that all the developers were in a single office, we owned every component we interacted with end-to-end, and the boss was across the hall and could be informed of anything pressing without much ado. I've also worked at fortune 500 companies which had multiple teams on a given service separated by vast amounts of space, in different times zones, and in such a case not having a unified service ticket system would have been absurd. I'll discuss ticketing in general in more depth later on in the book, but for now, suffice it to say, we need service tickets at most companies, and having an automated way of opening service tickets is quite useful.

Automating the ticket creation based on each and every alert will allow us to ensure that no technical debt is swept under the rug, and that we have meta-metrics about our application metrics. Such information, that is how frequently which particular alert was triggered, helps us to shape and prioritize our Serviceability goals with respect to addressing technical debt related to QoS and correctness.

What to Monitor

Monitors consume application state in the form of metrics, and allow us to apply a set of rules such that we are informed about impending or ongoing bad system states. As such, unsurprisingly, what we should monitor is largely an extension of what we need to have metrics on (though there are a few exceptions); namely, we need to have monitors on the ingress and egress points of our service, and our resources (CPU, memory, threads, GC).

Beyond that, however, there are a couple of additional considerations with respect to application health and general QoS that resource, failure, or latency metrics can't directly express, and which we need to monitor: the general availability of the application, and the call volume.

While the metrics we've defined so far are an excellent way to make sure there is visibility into the state of the application, none of those metrics are able to tell us if the service is down all together. This is where the "isAlive" monitor comes into play. Essentially, this is a simple ping of some URL associated with our service which returns metadata about the health of internal services and so forth. periodically, some external service should attempt to ping our SaaS, and alert the on-call if the service cannot be reached or the ping endpoint returns metadata indicating the service is not in good health.

Another scenario which our service's metrics are not capable of expressing in and of themselves is the case where we are not receiving the expected volume of calls. While the "isAlive" check is able to tell us if our application is capable of servicing requests as expected, it is not capable of telling us the general state of the call flow which leads to our API.

Consider the scenario where some defect or network issue is preventing the communication between service B and service C. Alternatively, there could be a gateway issue much higher up in the network stack where we have no monitors.

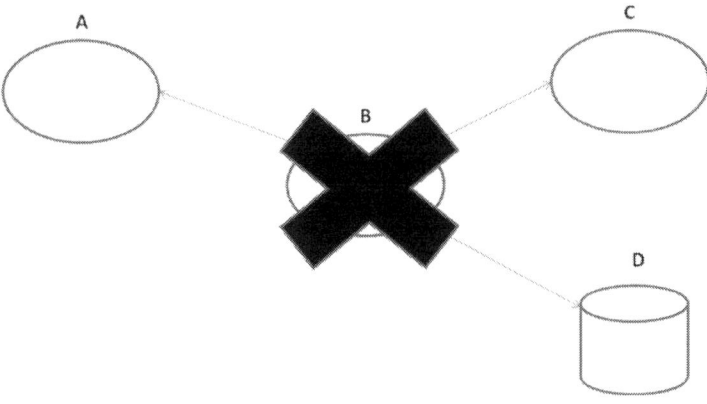

In this scenario, the "isAlive" check would communicate directly with service C. As a result, the "isAlive" check would find that service C is online and capable of servicing requests as expected, so no alert would be sent. If we had a monitor that informed us when our call volume was below a certain threshold value for a certain amount of time, we could be informed if there were some network issue, or other defect that prevented services from reaching us.

Beyond these couple of odd scenarios, however, we'll be applying monitors on the basis of our previously established reductive reasoning: ingress and egress points of the service, and general resources. That is, we'll apply rules such that all of our buckets of failures have an associated rule which will inform us if an API isn't satisfying QoS or correctness expectations.

How to Monitor

There are competing and varied schools of thought on the best way to approach monitoring, and a lot of depth as well. I've my own opinions based on experiences with a variety of approaches, and I'll expound upon the virtues of those in a moment. First though we should outline what it means to send an alert, and what precisely we expect.

An alert, by definition, is intended to get the attention of an on-call engineer. The expectation is that any monitor we've created has an expressly defined purpose, and reason for existing. An alert based off of a monitor needs to result in the ability of an on-call engineer to take a mitigating action to restore QoS or correctness.

On Apdex for Monitoring

A reasonably recently proposed solution with respect to the actual mechanism we use to implement our rules has emerged called "Apdex". I've worked with systems that utilized Apdex measurements before, and have a few gripes about it. In order to understand what I believe are shortcomings of the approach, we'll first need to have a basic understanding of the principle.

$$Apdex_t = \frac{SatisfiedCount + \dfrac{ToleratedCount}{2}}{TotalRequests}$$

$$t = targetResponseTime$$

The Apdex calculation results in a number between 0-1, with 0 being no requests were satisfied and 1 meaning 100% of requests were satisfied. A request is considered to be "satisfied" if the request response time is less than or equal to target response time, t. A request is considered to be "tolerated" if the response time r is less than $4t$; that is $t \leq r \leq 4t$. Any error return codes or response times greater than $4t$ are not included in the numerator. This is how we arrive at the Apdex value.

The general argument for Apdex is that it simplifies application monitoring, and measures what is important to the end user as well as the engineer. Tools that utilize Apdex will typically use a simple request interceptor, and auto-magically instrument the latency and error codes of the request. This in contrast to the metrics driven approach I've outlined in this book. While it is true that the Apdex equation is quite simple in that you merely need to supply a target time t, and you'll get a ratio, it makes a lot of assumptions, and misses the general principles I value most in my alerts and monitors.

First and foremost, the alerts which Apdex generates are by their very nature, quite ambiguous. An alert set to inform an on-call engineer based on an Apdex score being .7 or below for example could be a result of 30% of all requests having a hard failure (HTTP 500, 403, etc.), or, it could be 60% of requests being "tolerated" that is $t \leq r \leq 4t$, or it could be that 30% of requests are taking more than $4t$ in other words $4t < r$. In the best case, I have 3 scenarios that can cause my monitor to send an alert.

This violates one of the most important tenants of our overall Serviceability framework; namely reducing mean time to recovery by way of disambiguating the source of alerts. Alerts from Apdex driven monitoring tools do not meaningfully inform the on-call engineer about the specific cause of an error. Rather, they give a general, vague idea about what happened, and as an on-call engineer, I would still then need to manually examine my graphs and logs.

If the goal was to collapse the layers of the Serviceabilty framework, they've failed. We still require all the manual steps, and metric instrumentation, because the interceptor in this case did not express the exact response code, nor did it give a precise idea about why I received an error. Given that I need to manually examine my metrics graphs and logs anyway, seems I still need to implement those, and as such, the only real difference in savings in terms of development effort comes on the creation of rules for the sake of alerting via our monitors.

Other issues with Apdex related frameworks in my experience are that engineers unfamiliar with monitoring and ops duties in general tend to apply a universal Apdex policy to a service. Meaning, a hard policy that all the APIs of a given service have the same requirement for request response and error codes. Can we reasonably expect that a DELETE or HEAD call should take the same amount of time as a GET on a large amount of data? Can we also assume that all errors are equal, that is an error on loading an on screen ad banner is the same level of criticality as a database returning junk results? Such assumptions and propositions are absurd.

The general principle of reducing complexity of the monitoring framework, and reducing implementation time by using an Apdex interceptor rather than simple slope functions on metric data is a deeply flawed and misguided idea in my opinion. Implementing a simple interceptor in your own Service's code is not a monumental effort, and will give you appropriate, fine grained control of the metrics the application emits. This will allow for all alerts issued by application monitors to be meaningful, actionable, and in line with the our stated Serviceability goals.

We should never, ever look for shortcuts when implementing a Serviceability framework. The overall reliability and Serviceability of your application is of paramount importance, and without the ability to expediently triage and repair your SaaS, you have issues much more major than a slightly more complex Serviceability framework. We should do as much as possible ahead of time to prepare for the inevitable downtime event, not try to save a few dev hours by using an ill-fitting Apdex solution.

Basic Trigonometry for Monitoring

I've aired my grievances about Apdex, so now I'll discuss some general principles that can be used to catch bad system states using your metrics and some simple math.

First, let's discuss why static thresholds are bad. Given that we are owners of elastic SaaS that presumably also have varying request loads, we want to also have dynamic thresholds for our alerts. That is, we don't want to say "if

ERROR more than 5 alert me". Simply put, static thresholds make the assumption that request loads don't vary.

Request loads vary tremendously throughout the lifetime of the SaaS. As more and more users flock to your unbelievably awesome SaaS, your call volume increases, and as your SaaS becomes a dinosaur you are starting to phase out in favor of the next slick thing, your request load declines. On a less glacial time scale, during the course of any given day, your SaaS' call traffic volume will vary as well.

As SaaS owners, we accept that some requests will invariably take longer than expected, or return an error code for some reason or another. However, the rate at which we accept those failures will happen is very low, and we have hard QoS and correctness goals which reflect this expectation. If we have a static threshold of tolerance for 5 HTTP 500 response codes, does that same goal apply from to all times of day, all times of the SaaS' lifecycle? Certainly not!

At 10,000 requests, 5 represents .05% request failure, at 100 requests it represent 5%. Certainly these are dramatically different scenarios in terms of criticality of the system state, and the expected response of the on-call engineer. As such, we necessarily require a dynamic threshold for our SaaS' monitor rules. Such a rule is actually quite simple to create.

For any given API, we have buckets of metrics representing failures and errors, as well as a bucket that represents success. Thus, we can aggregate the occurrences of given types of return codes of a certain time window, and create a ratio of the failure state in that manner. I typically like to roll my metrics up into one minute windows. For fooBar API, we could create a simple ratio:

$$totalFooBarRequests = foorBar.error + fooBar.fail + fooBar.success$$

$$fooBar.errorRate = \frac{fooBar.error}{totalFooBarRequests}$$

Now I have a function that yields a result which is meaningful at any request volume.

Some sorts of simple rules I might derive using such a function could be:

if(max(fooBar.ErrorRate) > .01) over last 5 minutes, alert "fooBar.error exceeded local Max!";

Some other simple trigonometry can help to generate meaningful preemptive warnings as well. For example, we can use a simple slope function between two data points to determine if latency is increasing:

$$fooBar_{t1} = fooBar.latency.avg @ 22{:}00 \text{ to } 22{:}01$$

$$fooBar_{t2} = fooBar.latency.avg @ 22{:}01 \text{ to } 22{:}02$$

$$fooBarLatencySlope = \frac{fooBar_{t2} - fooBar_{t1}}{x_2 - x_1}$$

Now I have a simple slope function I can use to see if the overall trend of my latency is one that is increasing:

if(fooBarLatencySlope) > 0 for 3 datapoints, alert "fooBar.latency increasing!"

Slope functions are a great way to get out ahead of impending bad system states.

So the general principle is to apply some basic trigonometry and simple division to generate meaningful numeric values. Those values, in turn, can be fed into whatever particular rule set you're generating for your monitoring framework.

The specifics are a bit more nuanced, but in general, you'll want to have local max functions to catch breakout errors, and slope functions to give your on-call ops psychic powers. This will help ensure you find any breakout bad system states, and also give you a goodly amount of lead time via warnings if things are headed in the wrong direction. More specifics about threshold hysteresis, documentation, and so on will be discussed in the "Alerts" section of this book.

Now that we've examined the basic requirements for our monitoring rule sets, we should be well equipped to determine if a given monitoring implementation is well suited for use in our SaaS' Serviceability tool chain. Some key things to look at when choosing a monitoring tool are its ability to support the aforementioned mathematical equations in its rule sets, as well as its ability to support aggregation of data points for the purposes of creating rules based on trends which will require temporal relationships between data points be preserved in some manner.

Alerts and Alerting

Alerts are the last stage of the pipeline with respect to the expression of your system's state. Ideally, your monitoring framework is agnostic of where rule violations send alerts, and whatever consumer dwelling out in the ether can consume and catalog these alerts as they see fit. However interesting and numerous the use cases you find for your alerts are though, we have a pretty good idea what we intend for them to do as a primary function.

Alerts are the health monitor code-blue of your SaaS. Consider the line graphs, histograms, and pie charts to be the steady, pretty looking display you're occasionally entranced with, and alerts to be the flashing light and shrieking siren sitting atop the proverbial EKG machine. An alert's sole intended purpose is to get the attention of qualified individuals to prevent a catastrophic unexpected system state from persisting any longer than necessary.

If we can keep the purpose of the alert singular, and make sure to focus on this single intended purpose, we can avoid attaching unnecessary complicating elements to our alerts. Conceptually, we now have an understanding of what alerts are by virtue of what they must do. In terms of the theoretical implementation, we saw some simple examples of rules we could apply to monitor output in order to generate an alert in our monitoring section.

We'll expand on the use of rules, and specifics about their implementation. Additionally, we'll discuss the types of alerts to place on specific sorts of monitors, and some other meta-rule considerations. Beyond the nuts and bolts of the implementation of the rules, we'll also need to consider how these rules may be unintentionally violated and subsequently trigger alerts in the absence of an actual downtime or degraded service event.

What to Alert On

There are few major categories of alerts we want to have, and a few stray cases. The main cases that we want to alert on are the average, that is an aggregate value over a given time interval; the max or outlier cases, and the trend also known in graph lingo as the slope. Other simpler cases include the "isAlive" alert that lets you know your SaaS is not responding, the low network traffic alert which informs you there is some problem higher up in the food chain that is preventing customers from reaching you, and general resource metrics that will typically represent simple static thresholds, but may occasionally also consider slope.

Alert Suppression

The need for multiple types of alerts per monitor is another reason that it is handy to have the ability to suppress alerts. We'll explore the need for having multiple alerts for each of your monitors later, but let's discuss why receiving multiple closely related alerts can be detrimental to reducing mean time to recovery from bad system states.

 Imagine you've just been paged because the average rate of errors on your API "getFooBar" has exceeded your rule's thresholds. It is late at night, and you're half awake, staring at your computer monitor trying to figure out what is happening. The initial page is for your slope function, telling you your error rate is increasing. About 5 minutes in, you receive another alert, in the form of a jarring siren from an analog beeper. You drop everything, and attempt to gather at least a superficial assessment of which of the alerts you've received is the most urgent. After a couple of minutes, you realize it is an alert for the same API you're already triaging, letting you know the average rate of errors has exceeded your configured threshold. Still later, you receive a third alert for the maximum error rate over the last 3 data points having been exceeded.

Receiving multiple alerts forces the on-call to context switch, and drop their current line of thought on the primary reason they were paged. This leads to an increase in mean time to recover. If the API is part of a chain of dependencies in your SaaS' micro service architecture, the effect can be amplified further, and multiple alerts can fire at inopportune times in the triaging process.

After sending an ACK to these alerts, most monitoring and alerting frameworks require some additional updates to avoid triggering their escalation policies (more on escalation policies later). As a result, in addition to the initial context switch and time waste, the on-call engineer also has to periodically stop what they are doing and add more notes to the other related open alerts. Worse still is when you are so busy putting out the actual fire, you forget to add a note to an unresolved alert, and its escalation policy kicks in, paging other engineers unnecessarily.

While you might be apprehensive to the idea of silencing the alerts you've worked so hard to create, odds are the second and third such alerts carry little value to the on-call that is already on the case. We'll discuss making an official plan of action later, but in most cases, the first thing an on-call engineer will do is examine the visualization tools associated with the offending API. As a result, the engineer is already aware of other abnormalities with the API's performance, because they've already begun to analyze the graph and log output associated with the offending API.

You don't necessarily have to completely silence the follow on alerts, but they should not generally be disturbing an on-call engineer that is actively working the related alert. You might for example, have the follow on alerts only display as a flashing icon on your API's visualization page, or send an email. At that point, your on-call is waist deep in log output, staring at headers in Postman, and processing graphs in their peripheral vision on monitor number two. Likely, they've already found some forensic clue about what the alert is hinting at. Any jarring disturbances at that point can, in my experience, really negatively impact mean time to recovery.

In the ideal case, you'd have a sophisticated framework that would conditionally suppress the follow on alerts. Additionally, you'd ideally like to have the follow on alerts which are suppressed self-resolve within a window after the alert which suppressed them was resolved. That is, if the initial alert which is associated with the follow on or "redundant" alerts is resolved, the follow on alert should have some intelligence to check state again, and self-resolve if the state no longer exists. Self-resolving alerts can also be problematic however.

In the not so ideal case, you may have to cobble together your own framework. If you have some other restrictions relating to legacy infrastructure, you can reduce the total number of alerts. Although not ideal, in many cases, you can keep the total number of associated alerts lower by a factor of one or two by simply allowing the internal calls to dependent services to be subsumed by the API metric's alert.

Since we've accepted our reductive logic that most latency

and failures come from ingress and egress points, we can take it a step further. If an API has a metric, monitor, and alert at the ingress point, and that API is sufficiently instrumented such that it can express any internal failure as a total failure of its own state machine, we can then let the outer API's alert serve as the total alert.

There are some caveats here. We must be confident that the general exception handling around the API's interactions with any dependent services will be propagated such that the failure will be expressed by the overall API failure metric, and also still require that the dependent service interaction be instrumented with metrics. Additionally, in cases where your API interacts with multiple services to produce a response to the consumer of the API, the option to subsume the dependent service alert into the overall API alert can lead to an increased mean time to recovery due to the lack of specificity of the alert.

In the ideal world, you can have alerts at multiple levels in the API, and for each interaction with a dependent service. However, you can get away with subsuming dependent service alerts in the overall API alert in less complex use cases if you are comfortable with the ambiguity of the alert, and still have the ability to view metrics regarding the dependent service's interactions with the overall API functionality.

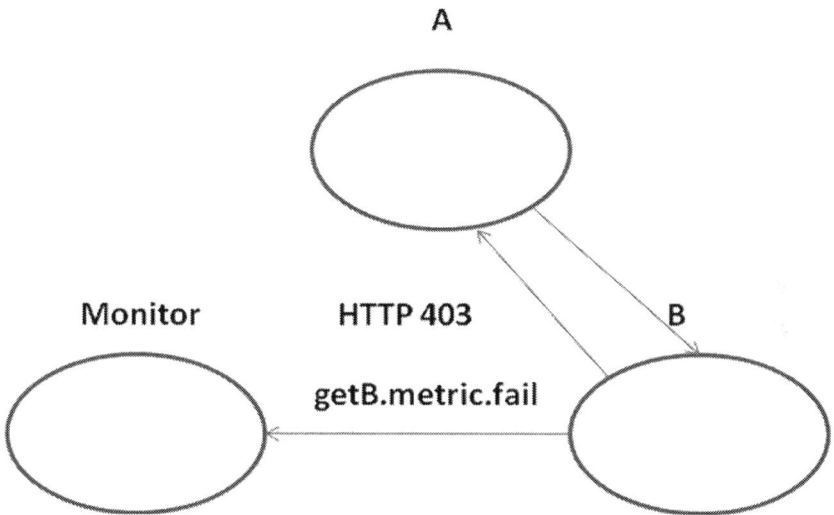

In a case where A depends on B, and B returns a 403, we send a failure metric to the monitoring software, but do not trigger an alert.

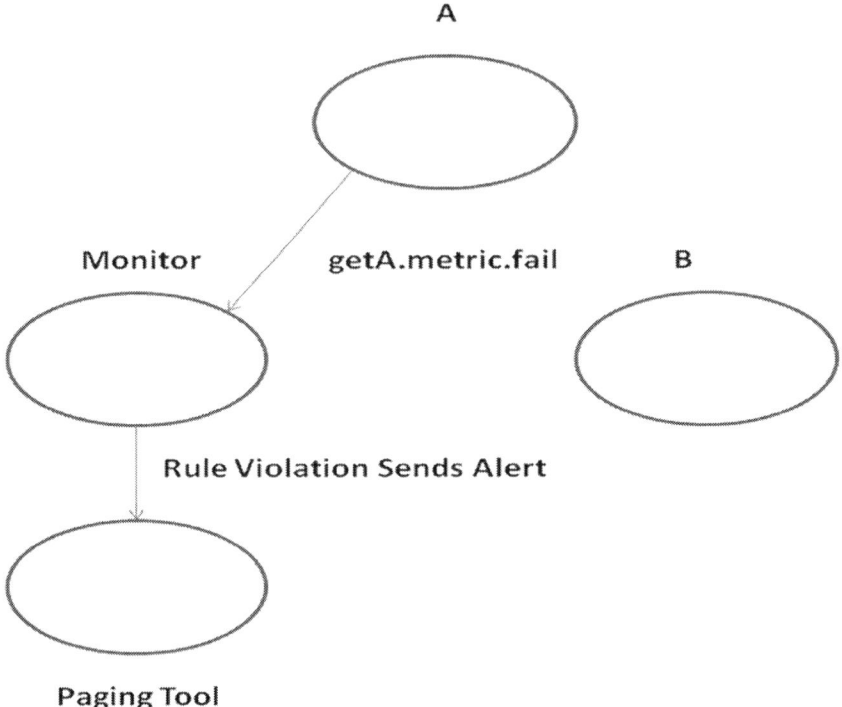

A

Monitor   getA.metric.fail   B

Rule Violation Sends Alert

Paging Tool

Instead, we fail the overall API interaction with A, send a metric for it, and subsequently send that alert.

In this way, we preserve the ability to investigate the interaction with the dependent service while also reducing the number of alerts we send to our on-call engineer. Again, this is not the optimal approach, as this alert is somewhat ambiguous. The alert could be caused by interactions with some component of the scaffolding that handles the request at the validation level in service A prior to getting passed to service B for example, but if you can satisfy the aforementioned conditions, namely preserving discoverability of issues with dependent service interactions by way of metrics, it will do in a pinch.

Alert Severity

The general idea behind alert severity is that alerts which are triggered by rule violations have differing implications with respect to the underlying system state, and as such, require different sorts of mitigating actions and also require differing levels of urgency on the part of the on-call. The spectrum ranges from a general warning of an impending bad system state to a severe alert indicating the system is not serving requests or responding to an "isAlive" check.

The class of warning alerts are related to our predictive formula which either utilize simple extrapolation via slope functions or indicates the approach of our metrics to the upper bound thresholds of our acceptable QoS standards. Violations of these thresholds represent the potential for an undesired system state to happen in the immediate future. While useful, and often accurate, due to the reliance on extrapolation rather than observation, these alerts are not foolproof. As such, we should consider carefully how we use these alerts with respect to when we page an on-call.

Generally speaking, it is my preference to only page on warnings during business hours due to the potential for inaccurate predictions. If, however, you have your extrapolations dialed in, and they are predicting oncoming bad system states with frightening accuracy, then by all means turn the alerts on 24/7.

Beyond the warning classification, there is a lot of general bickering about how to stratify the remaining hard QoS violations. In my estimation, it doesn't particularly matter if you classify an alert as "severity 1" or "severity 2", but rather there are really only two classes of alerts, those that indicate impending bad system states, and those that indicate a known bad system state. Beyond this distinction, the rest is merely taxonomy used for post incident analysis, or occasionally during an especially severe event to sound the air raid siren and get all hands out of bed.

The stratification of alerts will matter once we've crafted a complete holistic approach to Serviceability, but we can retrofit our severe alerts with some general ranking system after deciding that later. For now, the only important thing with respect to alerts is that we understand the differences between predictive and indicative alerts.

Pre-production Versus Production

The general manner in which we broadcast our alerts to our on-call engineers should take into account the origin of the alert. That is, we should consider whether the alert originated from a pre-production or a production environment. In the case of an alert from a production environment, the bad system state is affecting a real customer, where as in the case of the pre-production environment, the bad system state only has the potential to affect willing test subjects to include our alpha users, internal employees, and testers.

As such, we should reasonably have different considerations with respect to the urgency with which we respond to pages originating from the various environments. In the case of our production environments, we need to respond to alerts at all hours of the day and night to ensure that no customers are adversely impacted by any unexpected system hiccups. In the case of our pre-production environment, we can simply mark a build as not ready to be deployed to production, so we do not have a need to wake an engineer up out of bed. It is enough to page them only during business hours.

Alert Types

Average Alerts

Averaging over a given time window is a good way to catch the generalized case of some reasonably significant portion of your metrics violating your QoS standards. Averaging is, of course, a simple process; we sum the value of a given metric for a set interval, typically a minute, and then divide by the number of requests to get the average value of the metric. In the event the metric's average value exceeds the threshold, you would page. As discussed in the monitoring section of the book, all metric thresholds except for resource metric thresholds and latency should be based on rates, not static numbers.

As with any other alert, you can create a warning level, and an alert level. That is, the warning level as the average value approaches the upper bound of your QoS standard, and the severe alert after the upper bound has been surpassed entirely.

Max Alerts

While average alerts are quite good at catching general trends with data, they can obfuscate issues with small numbers of requests experiencing QoS violations. That is, our outliers fall victim to the tyranny of the majority, and their little voices are lost in the hum of the crowd. Not being aware of QoS violations experienced by outliers can diminish our ability to predict impending bad system states, and also prevent us from finding issues with certain use cases.

Often times, prior to a system falling over completely, there are indications with a small percent of your requests. That is, there are prodromes of total system failure. We can follow one such case logically; imagine a small number of requests start to take substantially more time to process than expected , because of some intermittent network issue connecting to a database. As a result, a small percentage of your thread pool will not be released as expected. Network traffic starts to spike as part of your normal usage pattern for that time of day, and the issue begins to become exacerbated, with more threads being consumed, more memory being eaten up. At this stage, however, there are still not enough requests experiencing the increase in latency to trip your average monitors. Eventually, enough requests will begin to experience the issues that the average monitor is tripped, and you are paged.

Other instances where being aware of outliers may help to track down potential issues is with uncommon use cases. For example, on an ecommerce site, we had a max request latency monitor, and we found that when it was tripped, we also had an increase in our memory usage. We eventually tracked down the specific set of requests, and found that it was a web scraping script that was pulling every single price for every single item on our website. This lead us to the discovery that our web GUI would return an essentially endless array of pages for a search result if the text box's code was manipulated just so in a console. We were able to patch the vulnerability, and limit the number of pages that the search code could return.

In both of these cases, had we not had a max monitor, our average monitor would have missed these situations entirely. In terms of how to implement a max monitor, you can typically find an implementation of the 90th, 95th, or 99th percentile in most metrics frameworks. Simply applying the same sorts of rules to one of these metrics will give you the visibility you need into the behavior of outliers.

Slope Alerts

Slope alerts are a very primitive form of prediction. That is, we use simple extrapolation to determine the general trend of the metric. Slope alerts are very simple to implement, but will require some fine tuning. If you make the slope too sensitive, that is say, if my slope is positive for two data points, alert; then you're likely to accidentally page an on-call during the course of your normal business hours traffic.

Naturally, you would expect that latency for example would increase for a couple of data points as your general service user demographic starts their typical pattern, and your service goes from serving almost no requests to serving many requests. On the other side of the coin, requiring that your slope is positive for too many data points defeats the purpose of having the alert at all. If you wait too long to trigger a slope alert, it is likely your max or average monitor has already found an issue.

The general principle behind the slope monitor is to predict impending bad system states by using a slope function to plot the next predicted data point of a given metric's rate. Of course, in the context of errors, latency, and total resources used, a consistent positive slope is bad, as it indicates you are headed towards a lack of resources, a high latency, or a high rate of errors if the trend continues.

Miscellaneous Alerts

For general resource metric alerts, the use of simple static thresholds is fine. That is, if you know how much memory your instance has for example, and it is easier to use a static threshold to cause an alert when you only have 500MB of memory left, feel free to do so. However, it is still generally preferable to use a percentage if you're able, so you don't have to manually change your alerts if you happen to change the total number of threads your SaaS has available for example.

We'll also want a few other generic alerts: an "isAlive" alert that pages if the system cannot be reached, and a low traffic alert that will let us know if something in our client or our network is affecting the ability of the end user to reach our service. Both of these alerts can use simple static thresholds as well. It's a good bet if you can't ping your service for a couple of data points, it is down. It is also a good bet there is some major issue in the network, or with your client if you are not seeing any requests reach your service during what are generally busy hours for your service.

Other Alert Considerations

Initial Thresholds and Revisiting Thresholds

The derivation of your initial thresholds for alerts should be based on load tests run on the SaaS prior to introducing to the wild for end users. Additionally, there will likely be goals from product managers and other user experience experts to maintain certain levels of QoS, so you'll need to take those considerations into account as well; though the pie in the sky dreams of UX folks might need to deal with the harsh realities of network latency, we should do our best to consider and comport to the general user expectations, after all the SaaS pays our checks, and if user research says it will see more use if we get our request latency down, we should endeavor to do so.

We may, however, find after applying the thresholds we got from our load tests to our monitors, or attempting to comport to UX QoS specs that we are seeing a lot of phantom pages. That is, we may well see pages that wake people up out of bed, interrupt productive work, and end up being nothing but run of the mill expected variance.

Here we should be clear about the distinction between the use of metrics generally, and the use of metrics for the purposes of Serviceability. Although it is nice to be able to comport to certain QoS metrics, the violation of such metrics may not always represent the presence of an underlying bad system state. There are a million reasons why latency, error rates, and resource usage could be different than expected, and only a small subset of those require immediate emergency action. The use of alerts should be exclusively to alert an on-call engineer about emergencies with the system that are likely to lead to total system failure, or a system that is so badly degraded that it cannot serve requests in a timely manner.

We can, and should, draw a distinction between QoS and UX needs, and Serviceability needs. We can use our metrics to review the general performance trends of the SaaS, and then investigate ways to improve general request latency, error rates, and resource usage. These types of improvements are important to the product, but do not constitute actionable emergency situations that require the immediate response of an on-call engineer.

Performance improvements need to be approached in a methodical, deliberate manner after careful review of long term trends of a SaaS' performance and general usage patterns. After carefully examining these trends, we will be informed about what sorts of improvements would have the greatest impact, and equipped to begin to implement those changes.

Although it is generally acceptable to revisit thresholds , there is certainly a step too far. I've found that people tend to not care for on-call duty - I'm not one of them, I love solving a mystery, and if you're adequately prepared for downtime events, it can be a blast - and as such, tend to do whatever they can to not get paged.

 This can entail doing things like changing thresholds to be less sensitive, or changing other meta-alert settings to make the alert less likely to trigger. Due to the general tendency of engineers to not care terribly much for getting paged, it is important to have a transparent, recorded meeting prior to adjusting alert thresholds, and have clear, reasonable, logical reasons for wanting to adjust something. There of course will be exceptions, such as when someone has accidentally set a monitor to trigger on 1 in 10M requests failing instead of 1 in 10K, and you're being incessantly paged every five minutes; use commonsense.

Hysteresis

Often times, we will have a single data point that violates a rule. This can be for any number of relatively mundane and trivial reasons, such as a dependent service was resetting itself, there was a temporary network issue, our instances were beginning to reach request saturation and were in the process of spinning up new instances, and so on. These sorts of random system burps do not represent an impending or ongoing bad system state. As such, they do not qualify as emergencies which we need to alert our on-call about. We can borrow some concepts from signal processing to help solve the problem of noisy alerts triggering phantom pages.

In embedded systems, and at very low level, any computing device really; one of the issues we face is one of a rapidly changing signal state. While we think of binary logic on a conceptual level as being a representation of two distinct states, a zero and a one, in terms of the implementation, it can be a little trickier than that.

Consider that you have a logic gate that allows all 0s and disallows all 1s. Again, conceptually, this is simple; however, in implementation, 0s are represented by a lack of charge, and 1s by a positive electric charge above a certain threshold. In certain cases, there may be transient reductions in electrical charge of a minute amount. Does your gate allow this as a 0 value, consider this to be a 1 value, do nothing?

One of the ways in which we can eliminate or reduce noisy signals triggering a state change on our logic gate is via the use of a concept known as hysteresis. Some common implementations in physical form include devices such as Schmitt triggers. As we've done earlier when considering our graphs to be signals for the purposes of applying decimation when storing metric data, here again we will apply the same analogy, and apply hysteresis to our alerts.

The concept of hysteresis is one of considering system state in the context of its recent history when determining its current state. For our purposes, this recent history will be adjacent data points. We will not simply ask "did a metric's rate for a data point (typically an aggregate of a minute) represent a rule violation?", and subsequently trigger an alert. Instead, we will ask "did a metric's rate for the last X data points represent a rule violation?" and subsequently trigger an alert if the answer is yes. X will typically be between 2 and 4 data points, but your use case may vary slightly.

By considering the general history of the metric's rate, we can avoid responding urgently to transient issues that do not represent real downtime or degraded system states. In so doing, we preserve the general integrity of an alert, and thus, the urgency in the on-call's mind, as they have confidence the alert is informing about a real problem, and not just making noise at 2AM.

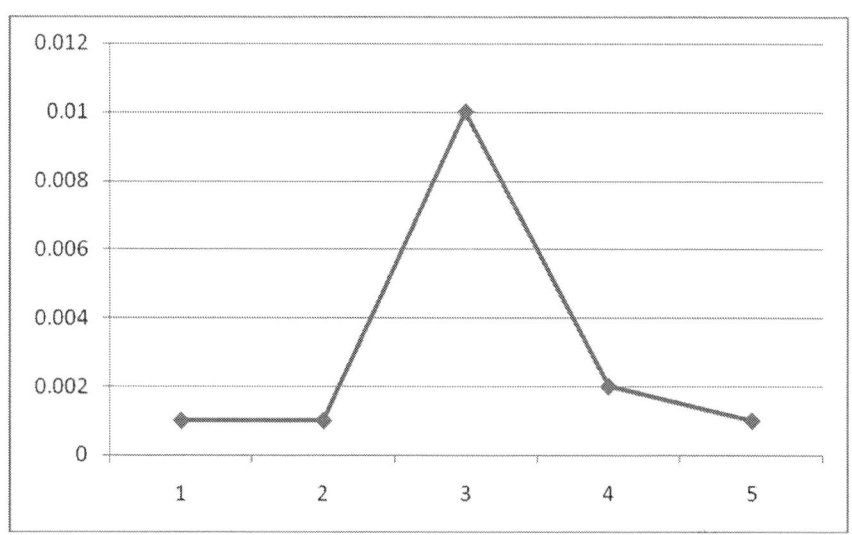

Single data point violation, don't send alert

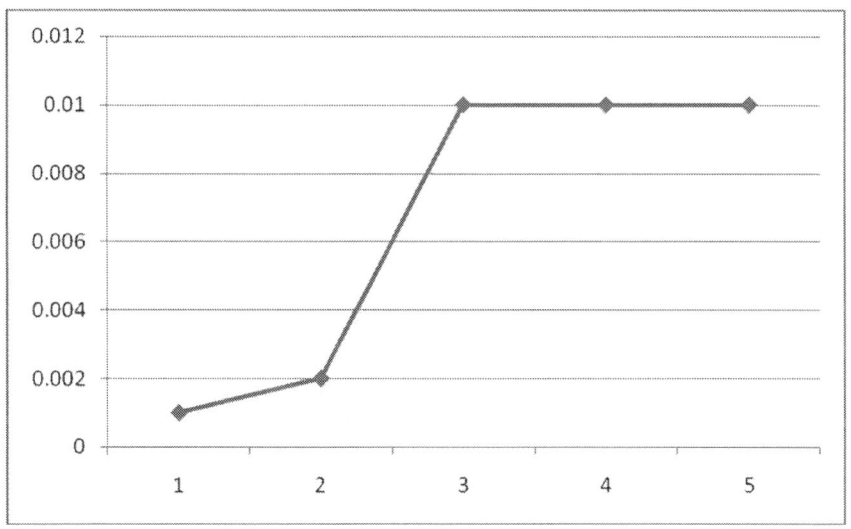

Consistent rule violation, send alert

We can effectively eliminate flapping alerts with hysteresis!

Resolving and Snoozing Alerts

Having a snooze ability on alerts tends to be a necessity,

especially in frameworks that do not allow alarm suppression based on dependency chains. During the general investigation of an ongoing issue, we don't want an alert to be constantly beeping at an on-call engineer, and if we have multiple related alerts, we don't want to get overwhelmed and confused while we investigate one or another of the issues. That said, snoozing an alert is another tool ripe for abuse.

Alerts should only be snoozed when you're actively investigating an issue, and are aware of the information the alert is presenting. I've seen abuse of the snooze feature such as hitting snooze and hoping the alert state is not present in 15 minutes, because the on-call felt it probably wasn't an issue, and it was late in the evening. I get it, I've been there, it sucks to wake up at 2AM and work some more after putting in a 10 or 12 hour day, but it comes with the territory. Just make sure your team has a clear understanding of the expectations with respect to snoozing, and that it is not used like the snooze button on your alarm clock.

Similarly, resolving alerts should not be done without a clear understanding of the core causes of the alert. Again, I've seen a lot of very non-scientific reasons for closing alerts based on general assumptions. Assumptions are the bottom of the barrel; you should never, ever be satisfied with an assumption. You should always endeavor to ideally have empirical evidence of a cause, or if that is not possible a very, very strong case built with inferential logic. I've been bit more than once early in my career by assumptions about the causes of issues, only to be woken up by another page a short time later; don't resolve unless you've solved!

Logging

Although well named, well placed metrics can help to disambiguate the source of an issue with your SaaS, they simply are not expressive enough that they are capable of discerning the exact underlying cause of a bad system state. We're able to reduce the search space with our metric, however, we still require that we have more verbose descriptions of the specific exceptions and other errors the SaaS is producing; this is where logging comes in to play.

While we don't want to have a lot of "got there" statements in an enterprise software system, we certainly need to be logging all exceptions, and also meaningfully describe any error messages. Without specific, detailed information about the underlying cause of an exception, we're left with having to rely on generalized assumptions; assumptions are pond scum in the world of computer science, always aim for empirical evidence, or in the worst case very strong deductive reasoning.

In addition to the general presence of logs, we require that we are able to isolate single discrete instances of interactions with the SaaS. We need to be able to isolate a single request within a given service, as well as that request's entire journey from its origin to its ultimate unexpected error state. As such, we need to have some kind of a unique identifier that follows a request from end to end.

Once we have appropriate logging of all exceptions and errors in place, and we have the ability to isolate single discrete interactions with a SaaS across various micro-services, we also need to be able to associate with a specific API. Once we've implemented some logic that allows us to isolate the interactions with a single API, we'll also need a consistent way to trace from the error backwards. That is, we'll need to start at the end of the journey of the request where the error began, and isolate that unique interaction.

Traceability

Traceability of a single discrete interaction with a SaaS is not as complex as it may seem at first. Whether the originator of the request is a web based JavaScript client, or a backend service in Java, the general approach is identical. The requester needs to generate a unique identifier via the use of a UUID tool, and associate that with all requests it originates. Additionally, if the service is not the originator of the request, it needs to pass the UUID from the originator to its dependent services.

If all clients and services comport to this general principle, it is possible to isolate a single discrete interaction with a SaaS in a very noisy multi-tenant environment. Multi-tenant SaaS serve many requests concurrently, and interact with a number of different dependent services. Without the ability to isolate a specific discrete interaction with your SaaS, it is extremely time consuming, and often virtually impossible to isolate the cause of a given exception.

Beyond the bare minimum requirement that each originator of a request include a general tracking ID with each request, other metadata can and should be included with each request as well. Often times, for example, we have errors reported from certain customers of our SaaS. In such cases, we would like to be able to isolate all requests from a given tenant (customer), and then go about reverse tracing from an error using the tracking ID. Any other such metadata that the originator of the request has at their disposal are candidates for inclusion as request metadata.

The implementation of such a system is not overly complicated. In the case of a REST service, the originator can simply include the values as known headers to whatever service it is interacting with. The receiving service, in turn, can use a simple filter pattern to auto-magically include these headers in the logs. Apache for example has the MDC or "Mapped Diagnostic Context" which accepts key value pairs, and includes them with every log entry. Similarly, you can have some general interceptor or filter that makes sure to include the request meta-data and tracking ID headers to any additional services which are queried.

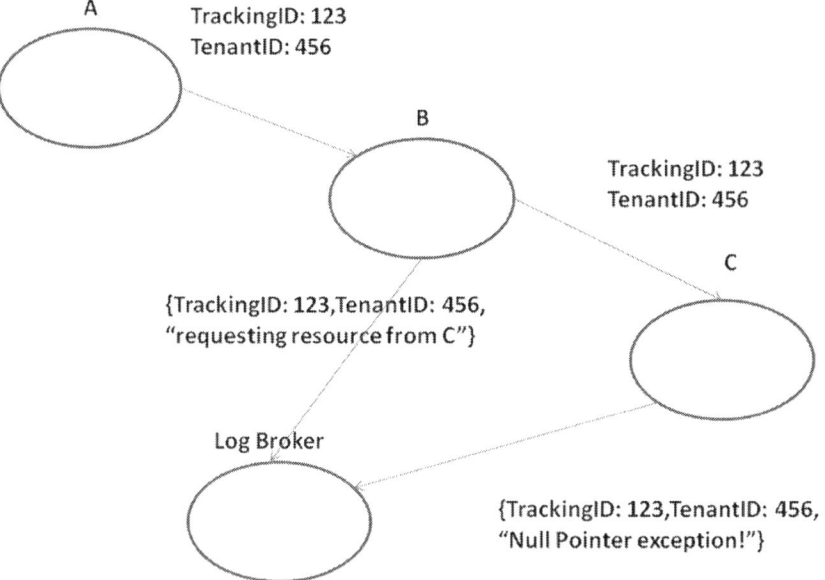

With appropriate request metadata included in logs, we can trace anything

Beyond tracking data used to identify a specific request, you should also place a unique identifier in the logs your service send to the log server that identify your SaaS. Consider that you will be sharing the log server with various other SaaS, so it is important to be able to isolate the log output of your specific service.

Isolating Errors

Once we have the request metadata schema worked out, all originators generate and include the data, and the request metadata is also included in the logging context, we can move on to how to isolate a specific API's errors. This is not actually terribly difficult. Since we've already implemented a meaningful metric naming schema, we can simply extend that and make some additional log entries.

Presumably, you're using some kind of a request interceptor, or other centralized module to send your metrics to whatever service it is that consumes the metrics for the purposes of visualizations, monitors, and alerts. As such, we should only have to add a small amount of code to this central module. All we are required to do is simply send a log entry with the metric name.

When we send a metric, say "getFooBar.fail" , to indicate a failure, we simply also write a log entry of the same. Due to the fact our request metadata is included with every log entry, we can now directly use the alert information to immediately find an instance of the API's failure. For example, if I receive an alert that states "getFooBar.fail exceeded threshold!", we simply create a filter in our logging framework to look for "getFooBar.fail", and voila, we now have our request metadata. From there, we simply use the tracking ID, and we now have the entire end to end journey of the ill fated request.

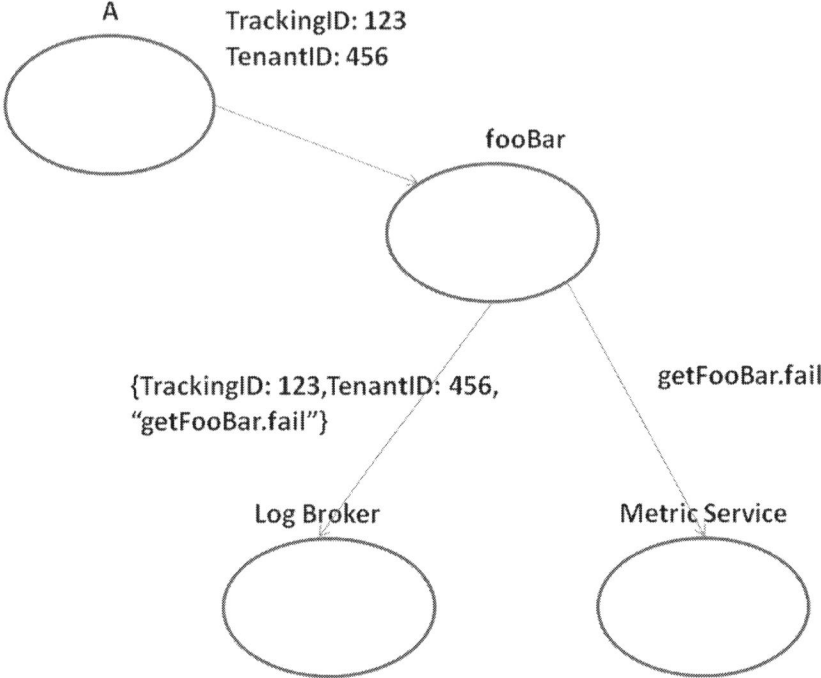

Simply log the name of the metric, and voila, you have the tracking info

Of course slight variations are fine. There are some metric frameworks that conflate the idea of a log and a metric, so if you are using one of those, feel free to just include the request metadata as necessary in your metric. The only important thing is that you are able to start with only the metric of the API, and associate that with the logs generated by the API during the failure case.

Log Implementation

I've worked with a variety of different log implementations. They ranged from very primitive raw text logs in tar.gz form to sophisticated multi-node data stores with their own query language. Irrespective of your implementation, you should have some queries documented and ready to go. There are, however, advantages to certain implementations over others.

Primitive log servers that simply toss your Tomcat logs and what not to some Linux directory are very simple to set up and manage. Additionally, you can easily tar and zip logs to increase the amount of time you can retain on a given amount of space. However, you're left with primitive tools to search these logs such as egrep. While egrep is an awesome command line tool, if your logs become too large, it is prohibitively slow for use as a tool to aid in the triaging process.

More sophisticated log solutions tend to be more complex to set up and administer, however, they are adept at what they do. Efficient custom query languages, and a GUI with the ability to create and persist visualizations based off of custom queries can substantially reduce your mean time to recover. Also, speaking from an on-call's perspective, I can say, it is a dream to use compared to raw text logs. I'll egrep some raw text if I need to, but I'd really prefer to have a visualization tool with more friendly query language.

Another consideration with respect to your logging is the time stamp. I'm honestly perplexed why not everyone in the SaaS business uses GMT for their logs. If you do not have a universal timestamp for your logs, then you can give your on-call a lot of headaches. If you are up late at night trying to solve an issue, and you have to go to a log server in a different time zone, you shouldn't have to do the math in your head based on the physical location of the log server to determine what timeframe to egrep for your request's journey through the SaaS.

Simply use a universal time zone for all of your log servers, and mandate that all of your clients also use a universal time stamp on their logs. This will make things much simpler for your on-call when it really matters. I can't even tell you how much time I've wasted searching for logs in some server in vain, only to realize it had a different time zone set, and the log entries I wanted were actually several hours in the future or the past; not a good use of your resources!

Implementation

I've intentionally made this book extremely light on specific implementation details in an effort to help keep the focus on general principles of Serviceability, metrics, monitors, and alerts while being implementation agnostic. As such, I won't add a lot of depth to this section. Given the rapidly changing trends in software, especially around the nascent cloud SaaS, it is not terrifically valuable to spend too much effort discussing specifics in terms of implementation.

If you're reading this book in the distant future, and we all have flying cars and what not, please forgive our primitive cave drawings. If you're reading this in the near term, enjoy musings on a smattering of tools I've used for Serviceability purposes. I'll hold my tongue on tools I don't think too highly of, but suffice it to say, I have tried a lot that made me curse the day I ever signed up for on-call duty; if it is commonly used, and not on the list, take that to mean I tried it and didn't care for it, or it didn't exist when I wrote this.

StatsD

This is a simple implementation of time series counters that is very bare bones. It is widely known and supported by ancillary commercial and open source bells and whistles. Setup is pretty simple, and most languages you will have occasion to use have robust, feature rich StatsD clients.

StatsD pushes simple metrics into a Graphite time series database. Dot notation in the metric name creates a file directory structure. So, for example "get.fooBar.fail" would create the directory structure get/fooBar/fail in Graphite. It is quite simple to send these lightweight metrics using UDP to a metrics collector behind a firewall in your private cloud. In this way, you can avoid too much of a performance drag on your application.

I really enjoy the flexibility of StatsD, and its general simplicity and robustness. Additionally, it is very focused on its singular goal of representing system state as plainly as possible, and in so doing, doesn't attempt to conflate the roles of logging and metrics. When sending UDP, you'll barely notice a constant stream of metrics in terms of resource usage; great tool.

Riemann

Riemann is a much more feature rich, heavy duty expression of system state. Where a StatsD metric is very thin, and simple, a Riemann metric is a kind of conflation of a log and a metric. It contains a goodly amount of metadata you would not necessarily expect, or frankly typically need from a metric.

The general principle is to create filters on streams of events, and subsequently also create alerts on those events. So rather than being a simple tool such as StatsD that only reports metrics, Riemann is an entire system that also includes logic to generate alerts and such.

Set up and configuration are non-trivial, and due to the verbose, heavy weight expression of the psuedo-metric, as well as the general resource intensiveness of crunching through that data, you can expect the Riemann tool to use more resources than lightweight UDP StatsD metrics. It does, however, offer alerting and such. However, I found that a lot of the functionality I wanted was difficult to configure, or just not really supported without some significant work.

If you're looking for an open source feature rich, all in one tool, you might consider it, but I'd be more inclined to start with StatsD, and layer your monitoring and alerting on top of that.

Grafana

Grafana is a great, simple visualization tool that is well liked, well supported, and has a a number of flexible features; it's also open source. Grafana can consume a number of different persistence stores, and has some great tools for generating graphs using queries which can be persisted in the form editable of dashboards.

Grafana can sit on top of most common persistence mechanisms you've chosen to store your metrics in, and make the raw data into histograms, line graphs, and so on. It is an invaluable and necessary tool for any serious SaaS, and did I mention it is open source?

Additionally, recently (December 2016), Grafana has added the ability to support alerts with Grafana 4.0. Can't say enough nice things about Grafana; love it!

Sensu

Sensu is a good intermediary for consuming event driven alerts, and also has support for writing Ruby scripts that are capable of forming the basis of an alert suppression framework. Although a little difficult to set up and administer, it offers powerful scripting capabilities that can be combined with other tools in your toolbox. Sensu can handle sending alerts to your end user as well.

 Is not a must have, but if you can get past the gruff exterior, and deal with the fact it is difficult to performance check your Ruby scripts, it is a worthy addition.

PagerDuty

PagerDuty is a robust, simple to use commercial service that can send SMS, TTS, email, and carrier pigeon alerts to your on-call when something goes wrong. It has a feature rich set of functionality that will let you design and easily implement different pager policies for different services, environments, and so on. PagerDuty also supports on-call scheduling, hunt groups and escalation to make sure your pages are never go unanswered.

PagerDuty is very well supported, and is essentially the de facto standard when it comes to alerting. Just about any alerting software you use can integrate with PagerDuty, and the mobile app is dreamy. While it is a commercial tool, it is bulletproof, and will save you a lot of grief versus implementing your own.

Kibana, Elasticsearch and Lucene

Elasticsearch is the persistence mechanism that first appeared in a colonnade of bright white light, bringing peace to on-call kind. No, but seriously, this setup is so amazingly useful. Elasticsearch is the distributed datastore for all of your applications logs. It efficiently stores all of the logs on multiple physical nodes, and allows for queries of very large amounts of raw log data to happen in a very tolerable amount of time.

While ES is not fast enough at querying this mass of virtually schema-less data to replace OLTP done by something like Cassandra, it is many orders of magnitude faster than running zgrep or egrep on raw logs.

Kibana is the equivalent of Grafana for logs. You can create and persist visualizations based off of queries written in the simple and flexible Lucene query language. These dashboards serve as a great tool to reduce mean time to recovery. You can have all of your Lucene queries queued up and ready to go for your on-call, so they will know exactly what tracking IDs were for all the errors from all of your APIs, how many of what particular return code, etcetera.

Kibana also supports a watcher that can send alerts, however, the syntax is a bit of a bear, and as you can imagine, these sorts of monitors are resource intensive. Additionally, the general somersaults and back flips you have to do in order to support the alerts via inserting log output in odd places is much less clean and simple than an interceptor that increments metrics. Feel free to give a few simple alerts a go if you please, but I would generally advise to keep alerting separate from your log visualizations.

Spring AOP

For the purposes of implementing interceptors, Java based Spring applications have a simple to use and flexible tool called Spring AOP. Spring Aspect Oriented Programming is an easy way to create various request interceptors that will wrap all of your methods, and ensure no metric is ever missed. You'll only have to use inline metrics for odd one-off cases.

Spring AOP uses simple key words such as "Around". For example, you can intercept all methods from a given class that start with "get" by stating "myclass.get*". Since we've named all of our API's ingress points appropriately, we can then use the "Around" keyword to start a timer, and then "Proceed" to let the function execute. When the function finishes, it returns to the AOP interceptor, and we can stop the timer, and use the return value of the method to determine success or failures. Then the metrics are sent via UDP via StatsD to a graphite DB; easy!

You can even sneak in a log entry with the metric name here for our old friend Kibana...

Meld

Similar to the Java Spring implementation, JavaScript also has a library or two to support AOP. Same case, different story, wrap a method, send the metric and maybe a log; easy!

Downtime Preparation

We've accepted that for a variety of reasons, we can expect that at some point our SaaS will inevitably experience a downtime or degraded service event. We've gone to great lengths to name our APIs meaningfully, and consistently; are logging all of our exceptions and errors, have added tracking metadata to all of our requests and log entries, are generating meaningful metrics at the ingress and egress points of our service, have monitors watching those metrics, have alerts that inform us of violations of rules we've implemented, and can quickly isolate single instances of any given failure in our logs.

Now that all of the scaffolding is present, and we have all of the appropriate visibility into our SaaS' state, we need to prepare a plan of action when the inevitable happens. This plan of action consists of several different components that will take advantage of all the work we've already done.

Homogeneous SaaS Ecosystem

I've proposed hard and fast rules about what various services should emit, and the specific naming schema that should be used. I didn't do this because I am generally eccentric, there is good reason for these rules. We want to do everything we can to eliminate the necessity of tribal knowledge. Tribal knowledge is the phenomena where you have to ask a person to be able to understand what a particular API does, what exceptions it might log, and what its general failure modes are; the old "go ask so and so, they know all about it!".

One way of helping to eliminate the need for tribal knowledge is by insisting that whatever the underlying implementation is, we all agree to abide by a common metric naming schema, and agree on some bare minimum metrics that every API must emit. The implementation is not important, we're agnostic there, but we require that we are able to understand the general emissions and error states of a given dependent service.

If your service is emitting an HTTP 401 for example, I can easily deduce that I am having some issues with the auth token I am attempting to use to access your service. Without a clear understanding of the metric being emitted by your service, and a clear way to isolate the logs associated with my request to your service, however, I would have to page your team member out of bed to sort things out.

This is not a good use of anyone's time, and if we happen to have bad documentation to boot, or a newer on-call, this could turn into a time consuming endeavor. Remember that our goal is to have well documented APIs, metrics, and general exceptions and errors in an effort to reduce mean time to recovery from down time and degraded service events. We don't have any particular religion about how your dependent service is implemented under the hood, but it must comport to some standards at the Serviceability level, or we've really invested a lot of effort to only be able to debug the internals of our own service, and that alone is rarely sufficient to solve a downtime event.

Virtually any sort of service is capable of opening a connection to a metrics server by virtue of being a cloud based service. The ability to communicate remotely with other micro-services is a prerequisite to be a dependent service in a cloud ecosystem, so we're not attempting to shoehorn in functionality where it doesn't belong. Metric clients are available for virtually any popular coding language, and on the off chance your particular off the shelf client doesn't do what you need it to in terms of metric naming, the implementation of a library or intermediary service is not overly complex. The client simply needs to be able to establish a connection with your metrics server, and push some lightweight datagrams. Low-level transmission protocols are some of the oldest and most mature components in our stack, so they are quite well documented, robust, and easy to extend.

Dashboards

The underlying system state expressed by metrics and logs is exceptionally useful, but in its raw form, can be difficult to consume and make sense of; especially in the wee hours of the morning. As such, we like to convert our SaaS' system information into a visual form that is easier to quickly assess. This typically involves using tools such as Grafana to create line graphs of our metrics, and tools like Kibana to generate meaningful histograms and distilled log output. The queries needed to create these views are simple enough, but having to get the necessary queries correct on the fly during an urgent downtime event is not something we want to have to do, especially in the middle of the night. If creating these graphs on the fly takes even just a few minutes, that is still an eternity to a customer seeing a "Service Unavailable" message. The customer can, and will choose a different vendor if we can't mitigate downtime events.

In the case of our metrics dashboards, we want a separate visualization for each API, and further, a separate visualization for errors and latency. Due to the drastically varying scales of latency and error rates, combining both measurements on the same graph can obfuscate the trends of the error rates of your APIs. Additionally, if you're paged for errors or latency rule violations, the first thing you'd be doing would be to look at the trends of those specific metrics. Further, if you're paged for rule violations associated with a specific API, the first thing you'll want to do is look at the general metric trends associated with that API, so including the metric output of multiple APIs in a single visualization only serves to make interpreting trends more time consuming.

The graphs should be mapped to the API in question, that is, the graph should be named after the metric that expresses the API. Here again, we're aiming to make discoverability of the metrics associated with a specific API simple. If you're paged for a rule violation based on a specific API's metrics, you should be able to take that information and directly do a grep of your metric dashboard page and find the visualization without any indirection. Additional layers of translation should be eliminated if at all possible. If there is some other abstraction present due to limitations with your metrics framework, make sure there is a simple lookup table that allows the visualization associated with the API to be found as quickly as possible; remember, minutes matter here.

Metrics graphs used for the purposes of triaging downtime and degraded service events should only include the last few hours of data. Most visualization tools have options to set longer timeframes if need be, but the less data you have to look at during your initial assessment, the better.

Log dashboards used for the purposes of triaging should distill your SaaS' log output down to specific error related information. Your log dashboard does not need to be as specific as your metrics dashboard. We typically only go to our logs after first examining our metrics dashboard, and have a general idea what we want to look for. If we've followed the implementation tips in the logging section, we'll be able to simply cut paste the metric name in our log visualization tool, and quickly find all the API's associated errors and exceptions.

Creating separate visualizations based on the error output of each API is also redundant, because we already have those visual representations in our metrics dashboards. Consider also that log servers consume log output from every service in your SaaS' ecosystem, and therefore have very substantial amounts of raw data contained therein. As such, filters you add to generate visualizations have a high cost in terms of resource usage.

As a general rule, you should not create persistent visualizations on your logging tool if the same purposes could be fulfilled using lighter weight metrics. Bringing down your log server is bad news. I've had to bring a SaaS back to life while our log server was down, and it was not a lot of fun. In addition to general performance concerns, these visualizations would also need to be accompanied by their associated log output, and such a setup would get very visually noisy and crowded on your GUI.

Use the logging tools for their intended purpose; namely to get access to the specific, detailed information relating to error states. Metrics are for the coarse grained expression and visualization of system state, logs are for finding and resolving the underlying causes of these bad system states.

The general filters you should have applied to your dashboard for logs should be pretty simple. Firstly, something that isolates log output from your specific service, as discussed in our logging section. This identifier will typically be some meaningful abbreviation of your service name, or your service name in its entirety if it is short enough. You may also consider some simple filters that isolate anything sent at an "ERROR" level from your service. This can short-circuit the search for issues in the odd case where you are not grepping for a specific metric name.

So to summarize, get very fine grained and specific with your metrics dashboards, and make sure you are using the API name to map to the associated visualization. Logs should be generally more coarse grained for visual simplicity, performance, and redundancy reasons. The high-level goal here is to capitalize on all of your hard work putting the metrics and logs in place in order to reduce your mean time to recovery.

API documentation

Commercial APIs and commercial and open source libraries, for the most part, tend to be pretty well documented. This is largely due to the fact that these APIs and libraries are designed for use by external actors, and those actors need an understanding of how they might utilize our APIs and libraries to help realize their business' ambitions. Naturally, they'll require an understanding of the functionality of these services and libraries in order to see if their uses cases can be fulfilled. Additionally, their technical staff will need detailed information about compatibility with various operating systems, support for legacy infrastructure, general performance, etcetera.

Unfortunately, when it comes to APIs and libraries for internal employee use to implement commercial products, I've found we often do not have the same concerns. The business case for the external customer is clear, but quantifying how we lose productivity and take longer to recover from downtime events is less cut-and-dried in the minds of many project managers and engineering folks. I've often heard the argument that in agile continuous delivery environments, we're changing functionality so frequently, and adding new features so often that documentation would drift, and become useless, so why bother.

I'd argue that because we add new features and change the functionality of APIs so often it is even more vital that we maintain documentation. Without a clear understanding about the current functionality of our dependent services, we're bound to forget to send a header, misconstrue something, or otherwise generally flub up our interactions causing headaches for customers and on-calls alike. The reverse is also true, that is if a service is making modifications to its own APIs, and checking that its consumers will be reverse compatible, they necessarily require an understanding of upstream services.

Of course, in a perfect world, we have end to end tests, change logs, and mailer lists that will catch any of these issues before they go to production, but we can't test everything and changes can slip by and go unnoticed until it's too late. Anything we can do to minimize the risk of failing an interaction with a service is worth doing. That entails documenting ,very specifically, what parameters your API requires, what exceptions it may return and why, and any other general information. For example, if your service will rate limit starting at X requests per minute per customer, or there is an upper bound on file upload size, or particular timeout settings, I need to know that.

Escalation Policy

An escalation policy is a policy your team, and the broader cloud ecosystem adopts with respect to what the expectations are for responses to alerts. The general idea is that we make sure that serious rule violations are not ignored, or inadequately addressed. An escalation policy accomplishes this by setting certain hard and fast rules about what amount of time an alert is allowed to be in an unacknowledged state, and how frequently an open alert's status must be updated with current information by the on-call.

In the event your primary on-call does not respond and acknowledge an alert within the agreed upon timeframe, the alert then pages the next on-call in rotation, or the next higher layer of engineering staff. Optionally, you may also implement rules that require an open alert's associated ticket be updated with some new information regarding the current state of the on-call's investigation. Requiring updates on the alert's associated ticket ensures that no one is simply hitting a snooze on the alert.

I've seen response time requirements ranging from 15 minutes to 1 hour. I think the sweet spot is somewhere between these two, but your mileage may vary. If you've used one of the common paging tools, they typically have support for escalation policies baked in, so there is a low cost of implementation.

Escalation policies, in my experience, are most effective when they escalate to the next level of engineering management. If escalation policies simply use a huntgroup approach, that is they page the pool of on-calls in rotation until someone acknowledges, it is easier for an on-call to justify not responding. Although with rare exception I've worked with other hard working engineers that took on-call duty very seriously, I've also had the misfortune of working with people that didn't. I'd end up getting paged in the middle of the night when it wasn't my on-call rotation, because these particular on-calls hadn't responded. They always had some excuse for why they weren't able to respond, or why they didn't think the issue was serious, and we'd have to manually gather all our engineering and incident notes to discuss with their manager just to get them to perform their expected duties.

 If on the other hand their manager, and their manager's manager, and so on are potentially going to be woken up and forced to deal with an alert, the sense of urgency and the consequences of not responding are more apparent. Generally speaking, the managers shouldn't end up getting paged, so it shouldn't inconvenience anyone. Managers also tend to like this approach, because they are able to stay on top of any engineers that need additional understanding imparted with respect to how vital on-call duty is for a SaaS.

On-Call Troubleshooting Document

The on-call troubleshooting document is some form of internally accessible Wiki-like thing. The purpose of this collection of data is to aggregate any and everything an on-call might need during an emergent downtime or degraded service event. While we don't want this document to become so long and noisy that it is impossible to find anything in a timely manner during a downtime or degraded service event, we do need it to be comprehensive, well organized, and above all, useful.

There may be a temptation to throw every and any bit of

information or thought about your SaaS in the on-call troubleshooting document, but resist that urge. While it is better to have and not need, there is definitely a point where there is too much raw information, and it becomes difficult to effectively use the document in a timely manner. I'll outline some specific pieces of information you should have on your document.

In addition, you should have a redundant copy of this document ready to serve from a different source. I've been in the nightmare situation before where the document's web server was unavailable, and I had to resort to relying on my web browser history to locate all of the necessary information.

As part of the general acceptance of a new feature, the introduction of a new dependency, or other refactoring of existing functionality, we should require that this document be updated as appropriate. Consider this to be a living document that will evolve and change as your SaaS evolves and changes.

Description of Service

This section is for members of other services that depend on your service. The description of your services should be concise, but descriptive enough to give someone a general idea about what role your SaaS may, or may not, be playing in an ongoing downtime or degraded service event. Write this section as if you knew nothing about your service, with the audience consisting of your peer engineers.

Team Member Information

A simple collection of your team member names, your

manager names, and anyone else directly knowledgeable about the project. A single sentence or two about area of expertise and role on the team is sufficient. Additionally, you should also have a non-urgent contact such as an email, chat-id (Skype, Spark, Jabber, Slack, etc.); and an urgent contact and backup urgent contact such as pager-duty alias and personal cell phone number.

The purpose of this section is to ensure that there is never a point where no expert in your SaaS is unable to be contacted. As an engineer on the team, you may need to consult with another engineer on your team, or a higher level technical manager to get urgent assistance. Other service owners may also need to contact members of your team with general questions about issues they are seeing in pre-production environments via non-urgent channels, or may need to get in touch with urgent escalations if the usual pager tools are not working.

Contact Information

While we already have contact information for individual team members, we also should have some general SaaS scoped contacts that are multi-cast to the whole team, or to the current on-call. The reason being we may have a general question, or we may have an urgent issue that should be handled by whomever the current on-call is.

The urgent team channel should be the pager-duty alias that will page the current on-call, and then the rest of the hunt group via your escalation policy. The purpose of this channel is to provide quick access to your on-call to other services that depend on you. Having this information readily available will cut down on the amount of time it takes to get the owner of the right service to start triaging downtime and degraded service events.

The non-urgent team channel would include your business hours paging alias, your team mailer, and any related "ask <your SaaS name>" chat channels you have (Skype, Spark, Slack, etc.). This channel is used to address concerns and issues in pre-production environment deployments, general API questions, and feature requests.

The inclusion of non-urgent contact channels on a troubleshooting document may seem a bit odd, but your on-call will also be fielding non-urgent issues during business hours. Rather than bifurcating things, since the non-urgent and urgent issues all flow towards production customers if not addressed, we simply include them in the same documentation.

Current Open Issues

Whatever issue tracking system you are using, there should be some simple stratification which can be easily used by an on-call to determine the level of urgency required. The top level, most urgent events might be "Severe" for example; indicating an ongoing customer impact that requires immediate attention. Any such events that directly affect customers or consumers of your service need to be prominently displayed, or accessible via your troubleshooting page.

During ongoing emergencies, it is necessary for consumers of your service to be able to quickly assess if you are already aware of and working on an ongoing issue (this is especially true if you do not have alert suppression available). If an on-call for a service which depends on you sees that you already have an open ticket for the incident, they can link to that ticket in their own open issue, snooze or close their related open alert, and head to bed, or offer to help if you need it.

Without visibility into the issues with a service, consumers of your service, and other personnel that route customer issues are likely to open new issues, and each of these will urgently page you while you are in the middle of trying to solve a serious downtime or degraded service event. Additionally, if consumers of your service don't see an open issue on your service they may waste time and effort trying to track down the issue on their end of things.

For non-urgent issues, such as pre-production found bugs, it is also useful to have visibility. If for example your latest build introduces a bug that affects multiple consumers of your API, those service owners can do a quick check to see if there is already a ticket open to resolve the issue. They can then subscribe to updates on the ticket, add comments indicating their service is also being impacted, and so on. Without this visibility, you are likely to get multiple business hours pages and multiple tickets for the same non-urgent issues; this is not a fun thing to wade through, and is generally a waste of everyone's time.

Links to Metrics, Log Documentation Troubleshooting Instructions

You'll want to have links to the lookup tables you've created for your metrics as described in the metrics and logging sections. This aids the on-call by allowing them to quickly decrypt the meaning and potential impact of an alert associated with a given metric. You may also have some troubleshooting tips in a column of the lookup table.

These tips should be relatively brief: a list of interactions the metric has with respect to persistence stores, caching mechanisms, and dependent service APIs; and a couple of general steps the on-call can follow to eliminate or verify the cause of an issue. Consider our metric documentation from our metrics section, and add an additional column to describe the dependent services and troubleshooting steps:

Metric Name	Usage	Associated API	Dependent Services and Tips
postCustRecord	Create customer record in DB	ourService/api/ v1/CustRecord	<Link to document>

postCustomerRecord Dependent Services and Troubleshooting Tips
Depends on: SQL DB, getfooBarBaz API, authentication server
Troubleshooting: for 401 and 403 HTTP return codes, check health of authentication server. 404 HTTP return codes, check if record exists in SQL DB or getFooBarBaz service interaction. 5XX HTTP return codes, look for timeouts interacting with services, or general coding errors.

No troubleshooting document can be comprehensive, and you shouldn't aim to be. Your on-call engineers need to be able to use deductive logic, general computer science knowledge, and troubleshooting experience to deduce and confirm what the source of the problem is. However, there is no harm in giving some general tips, and it is definitely a must-have to know what services and persistence stores a given API interacts with.

Links to All Dashboards

This requirement is very simple and straight forward; simply link to all of your service's log and metric visualization tools. On-call engineers will look at these visualization tools as the first step in any troubleshooting process to examine general trends with the API's behavior.

Links to API Documentation

Again, a very straightforward requirement, simply make sure to have links to all of your API documentation we created for your service earlier. API documentation can be useful to other services that consume your APIs. Having access to this information may give them enough information that they are able to solve client side errors on their own, without having to wake up your on-call.

Additionally, API docs can serve as a refresher for engineers that may not have worked directly on a given API. There are also APIs that are generally stable, or are legacy APIs that haven't been modified in a long time. Such APIs will likely be less familiar to newer engineers, and having access to documentation will aid in troubleshooting, and prevent the need to page other engineers to solve issues.

Links to Build and Deployment Pipelines

Links to all build and deployment pipelines should also be

included in the troubleshooting document. Having these links allows consumers of your service to establish temporal relationships between the onset of failures, and the deployment of new versions of your service. Additionally, your own on-call engineer can verify, or dismiss a theoretical association between the onset of unexpected systems states and deployments of new versions of code.

One of the major sources of defective interactions between services and defects internal to a given service is the introduction of new functionality. As previously alluded to, in a continuous delivery SaaS we have relatively brief testing periods, and cannot hope to test all interactions anyway due to the inherent complexity of modern distributed systems. As such, it is always helpful to be able to check when your service, or services upon which your service depends last introduced new versions of their service to the pre-production or production environments.

Being able to associate failures with a new version allows for either a quick rollback to restore expected functionality, or a quick hot-fix. Without the ability to quickly associate when the latest version of a given service was deployed, we may not be able to quickly affirm or discount certain hypotheses during an emergency situation.

Links to Any Continuous Automation Testing

Similar to the requirement we have links to our build and deployment pipelines on our troubleshooting document, we also want to have links to any automated tests we have running against our pre-production or production environments. Having links to any continuously running tests will allow us to verify a temporal relationship between various other system states and the onset of our failure.

For example, if we see that an end to end test that runs periodically had been passing as expected all day, but began to fail suddenly, we can then cross reference that with the build and deployment pipelines, and see if new changes introduced may have caused an issue. Although this kind of temporal relationship is not empirical proof, of course, it can help to disambiguate the source of an issue and reduce the search space of our initial investigation.

Links to Dependent Service Documents

One of the great benefits of every SaaS in your cloud ecosystem adopting the general idea of an on-call troubleshooting document is that you can form a web ring. Essentially, once we have all of these awesome repositories of information in our internal wikis, we can link to all of our dependent service's troubleshooting documents in our own troubleshooting document.

We can then take advantage of all of the work other service owners have done. We can view their graphs, see if they have open high-priority issues, get information about how to contact their managers or team members for urgent or non-urgent reasons, see when they last deployed code changes, examine their API documents, and generally grep their service info in our downtime. Every service in your ecosystem should have an up to date troubleshooting document like this; no exceptions!

Dry Run

Once you've gotten your troubleshooting document put together, give it a try. Ideally, have an engineer on your team that was not involved in creating the document, or an engineer from another team give it a shot. We're interested in a fresh perspective on the document, and the general organization and comprehensiveness of the information provided.

Simulate a failure, and attempt to use the troubleshooting document to guide you to resolution of the incident. Exercises like this will help identify gaps in the document, and also serve to prepare you for when a real incident happens; you don't want to be looking at this document for the first time at 2AM trying to triage a real customer impacting issue. The troubleshooting document is a living document that will need to be kept up to date, so periodic dry runs and sanity checks of its contents should be performed.

Made in the USA
San Bernardino, CA
03 February 2018